Financial Mail
on Sunday

Complete Guide
to Investing
Using the Internet

*Financial Mail
on Sunday*

Complete Guide
to Investing
Using the Internet

Matthew Wall

RANDOM HOUSE
BUSINESS BOOKS

Published by Business Books in 2002

1 3 5 7 9 10 8 6 4 2

Copyright © *Financial Mail on Sunday* 2002
(A division of Associated Newspapers Ltd.)

Matthew Wall has asserted his right under the Copyright, Designs and Patents Act,
1988 to be identified as the author of this work

First published by Business Books in 2002.

Business Books
The Random House Group Limited
20 Vauxhall Bridge Road, London, SW1V 2SA

Random House Australia (Pty) Limited
20 Alfred Street, Milsons Point, Sydney,
New South Wales 2061, Australia

Random House New Zealand Limited
18 Poland Road, Glenfield
Auckland 10, New Zealand

Random House (Pty) Limited
Endulini, 5a Jubilee Road, Parktown 2193, South Africa

The Random House Group Limited Reg. No. 954009

www.randomhouse.co.uk

A CIP catalogue record for this book
is available from the British Library

Papers used by Random House
are natural, recyclable products made from wood grown in
sustainable forests. The manufacturing processes conform to
the environmental regulations of the country of origin

ISBN 0 7126 8097 7

Typeset in Sabon by MATS, Southend-on-Sea, Essex
Printed and bound in Great Britain by
Mackays of Chatham PLC, Chatham, Kent

Contents

Author's Note

At times, writing this book felt like playing hide-and-seek with the Invisible Man. The threat of global recession, terrorism, and the subsequent collapse in investor confidence, created a particularly turbulent climate for internet investment services. As a result, the industry was, and still is, in a state of flux. Chapters needed updating as soon as they were completed. But a line had to be drawn somewhere. Luckily my editors were on hand to draw it, otherwise this book would never have been published.

So my thanks go to Clare Smith at Random House for her patience and understanding, and to her editorial assistant, Tiffany Stansfield for her cheerfulness and efficiency. I would also like to thank Mike Harrington at MATS Typographic Services for surmounting technical problems with the 'savoir faire' of a seasoned professional.

And finally, thanks are due to my wife, Wendy, for tolerating the bizarre nocturnal behaviour often displayed by authors under threat of approaching deadlines.

Matthew Wall

CHAPTER **1**

Introduction

Welcome

Welcome to *The Complete Guide to Investing Using the Internet* – a book for investment novices and experts alike. It helps you to take this new communications phenomenon by the scruff of the neck, harness it and make it work for you. We show you how to get started online and give you all the tools you need to begin building wealth and taking complete control of your finances.

The internet revolution has only just begun

The first point to make is that we are only at the start of the internet revolution. With the ever-increasing pace of change and technological development, we forget just how fast the internet has penetrated society. Just like the mobile phone, the web has become an integral part of our lives and many of us now take it for granted.

But less than ten years ago, hardly anyone had even heard of the internet. Now almost every major company has its own website, communicating with its customers and suppliers online, and conducting business electronically too. E-mail has proved to be a communications phenomenon – still the internet's most popular application. Over 20 million people now have access to the internet in the UK and the global figure is approaching 500 million.

And this is just the beginning. Most of us are still struggling along with 56kbps modems, waiting impatiently for web pages to download and watching jerky video images on our computers. But high-speed 'broadband' internet is being rolled out as I write, giving consumers access speeds up to ten times faster than conventional modems. This means that large software programs can be downloaded in a flash and 'real-time' video-conferencing using web cameras is becoming a reality. The whole internet experience is shifting up a gear.

As mobile phones and hand-held organisers merge, we're seeing a new breed of multi-functional gizmo that can store all our diary and address book information, give us access to e-mail and the web, and allow us to talk to people. In a few years' time the speed of the mobile-phone network will be greatly enhanced too, thanks to third-generation (3G) technology. This will allow far more sophisticated information and services to be delivered to our 'supermobiles' wherever we happen to be.

What all this technological wizardry gives us is unprecedented access to information and the ability to act on that information. It gives us greater control over many aspects of our lives, especially financial affairs. And the better informed we are, the more likely it is that we will make the right decisions.

The internet and financial services

The internet is ideally suited to financial services. Most money these days is digital – just numbers passing between computers at the speed of light. (In view of this it seems all the more ludicrous that it takes three or four days to transfer money electronically between banks. But that's another story!)

Investing, in particular, seems to have been made for the internet. Share prices and stock markets move fast, so it needs a speedy resource to keep up with them. Not only can you get live prices, news and market information online, but you can also put that information to good use instantaneously, buying and selling in a matter of seconds.

The internet and computers are superb at handling vast

amounts of data, sifting and sorting them in practical ways. The ability to see share price graphs, portfolio valuations and research information on one screen is extremely useful. Investors now have more control than they have ever had.

Investing online defined

Although buying and selling shares is the most popular online investment activity, you can also invest in funds, such as unit trusts and open-ended investment companies, bonds, futures and options, and many other types of investment.

Most online stockbrokers now offer 'real-time' dealing where your order is processed immediately without any human intervention. A few just accept orders by e-mail, process them manually, but still call it online dealing. This isn't as efficient as the fully automated variety. The problem is that you don't actually know the price at which you will buy the shares because of the inevitable time delay between your order being sent, received, understood and executed. It may only be a matter of minutes, but share prices can move significantly in that time.

Brokers that only offer e-mail ordering tend not to be very sophisticated in other areas of service too. There's also a greater chance of error when fallible humans are involved.

The rise of the online investor

So it comes as no surprise to find that growing numbers of investors are switching from the telephone to the internet. It is faster, cheaper and gives investors access to information whenever they want it. What's more, investors are no longer restricted to their own domestic markets. Increasingly, online stockbrokers are providing access to US, European and the Far Eastern stock markets. Private investors are being offered global investment opportunities from the comfort of their own homes.

There are around 350,000 online investors now, compared with around 50,000 three years ago. And with some 12 million shareholders in the UK, the growth potential for online investment

The rise and rise of the online investor

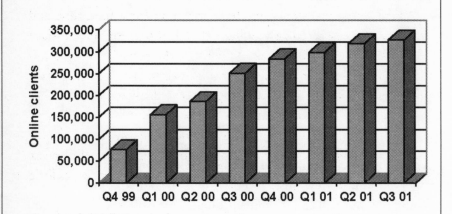

The number of online share trades

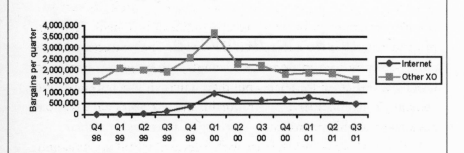

Bargains = share trades

XO = Execution only

Source: Compeer

is obvious. But not so long ago industry analysts were predicting an explosion in the number of investors trading online. The talk was of millions, not hundreds of thousands. So what has been slowing down the rate of growth? There are several reasons for this.

First, most investors have been investing for a long time and have grown used to a traditional telephone or face-to-face relationship with their broker. Many still like receiving advice and the human touch. Of course, there's a price to pay for this advice that is built into the cost of dealing. Internet brokers, on the other hand, tend to be 'execution only', which means they don't give advice. They compensate for this by providing online research tools to help investors make their own decisions. In return, dealing costs are much lower. Some online stockbrokers are now charging as little as £5 per trade for new customers.

Although the percentage of 'execution-only' trades made by private investors has risen to 30 per cent of the total, the rate of growth has been slower than expected because traditional investors have been a little tentative in entering this new self-sufficient environment.

Second, the investment industry has moved to electronic trading and settlement in the drive for greater efficiency. This means that most online brokers do not supply paper share certificates or contract notes any more. Investors make do with electronic confirmation notes, which they receive online or by e-mail. They can print these off for their records if they wish. Their investments are also usually pooled in nominee accounts, where investors remain beneficial owners of the shares but their names do not appear on the company's shareholder register. Again, many traditional investors have taken a while to adjust.

Third, as is so often the case with forecasts, world events simply knocked them for six. The demise of many high-technology and dot.com companies, the threat of a recession in the US and the terrorist atrocities in Washington and New York on 11 September 2001 have all contributed to a sustained period of investor fear and uncertainty. Investors lost confidence and almost stopped dealing completely.

According to the Association of Private Client Investment Managers and Stockbrokers (APCIMS), the main body for the UK retail investment industry, online trading activity dropped by a massive 21 per cent in the third quarter of 2001 compared with the previous quarter. Each investor made just 1.5 trades on average, compared with over six in the first quarter of 2000.

The sad truth is that many new investors were also trying the internet for the first time. They had their fingers badly burned when the dot.com bubble burst, lost a lot of money and retired hurt to lick their wounds. Once bitten, twice shy, they say. This tranche of investors will take a long time to recover.

Recovering from the dot.com bubble

The dot.com phenomenon needs some explaining because the internet has been unfairly tarnished as a result. During 1999 and early 2000 we were at the height of the technology stock boom that saw speculation run rampant and company valuations reach unfeasibly high levels. The problem was that no one – especially not the experts – knew how to value these new high-tech companies. The market valuations were based on assumptions about growth rates and the general take-up of technology on a global basis. It took the brooding clouds of recession in the US to prick this bubble once and for all.

As major companies reined in their spending on information technology in an effort to cut costs, so the wildly optimistic forecasts for high-tech companies appeared just that – wildly optimistic. But what people tend to overlook is that many of these businesses failed simply because they were bad concepts implemented by poor managers, assessed by financial analysts making pie-in-the-sky assumptions. Yet the high profile of these failures unfairly tarnished the reputation of the internet. In the bricks-and-mortar world of the high street 70 per cent of small businesses go bust within three years anyway. Commercial life is brutal whether you are online or not.

In the millennial year the US stock market's unprecedentedly long bull run was over and the champagne soon went flat. Investors were in a quandary. Should they cut their losses and buy back in later? Should they simply sit tight and weather the storm? Many did sell and buy back in, thinking the markets couldn't get much worse. They did, plunging through new lows each time.

In a volatile market, it only takes the whiff of trouble to send institutional investors into a panic, leading to heavy selling and sickeningly large share price falls in a matter of minutes. There is an infamous list of high-tech companies whose share prices have fallen by over 90 per cent from their over-inflated peaks. And the problem is that a lot of these companies may never recover. For many investors, simply battening down the hatches and waiting for better weather has only ensured total loss of their capital.

The year 2001 didn't prove to be much better. With the US Federal Reserve engaged in a drastic round of interest rate cuts to fend off looming recession, the markets continued to drift downwards, albeit at a less vertiginous pitch. Hopes of recovery were put back time and again. Profits warning followed profits warning, with many companies going to the wall. Venture capitalists lost fortunes, not to mention reputations.

Then, to cap it all, we had the terrorist attacks on the World Trade Centre and the Pentagon. Confidence hit a new low and recession seemed inevitable. All this turbulence has had an inevitable effect on the take-up of online investing. Many new investors have learned what they should have known already, but may never have experienced so dramatically: shares can go down as well as up.

The number of online investors may not be growing as fast as the pundits predicted, but it is still growing and will continue to grow. The technology is becoming more sophisticated, the range of services widening and the realisation growing among ordinary people that they have to provide for their own futures.

The internet: a health warning

But before we get into the meat of the book, take time to heed a few warnings. One of the side effects of instant access to information and dealing facilities is impetuosity. Accessing your trading account in a couple of minutes, receiving live streaming share prices, market data and company news is all very exciting and impressive. But the danger is that it goads us into acting when maybe we shouldn't act at all. Inexperienced investors – and I include myself in this category – can get carried away with the immediacy of it all and get swept up in the drama of volatile markets. Prices plunging and rising in seconds right before our eyes can induce a sense of panic – not the best emotion to inform investment decisions.

We deal with investment strategies in another chapter, but I think it is worth stressing here that the internet is merely a tool. It is not, by itself, going to make you rich overnight. The same principles underlying traditional investment decisions should apply to investments bought over the internet. That is easier said than done, of course. Sometimes it is better to do nothing at all, yet the accessibility of online dealing often tempts investors to tinker and dabble, usually resulting in impoverishment.

It may seem strange, in a book about investing using the internet, to be so apparently negative and cautious. But it is precisely because the internet is so effective that these warnings are justified. Making money from investing is not easy, as thousands of new investors have recently discovered. Highly paid City professionals were recommending that their clients buy shares in companies that have since plummeted in value. If they can't get it right, why should the novice investor be expected to?

What type of investor are you?

The most important thing to do before investing online is to decide what type of investor you are. It will make a big difference to the way you use the internet. There are two main types: investors and traders. Investors invest for the long term – a minimum of five years, say – basing their investment decisions on fundamental analysis of growth prospects of the underlying companies. They are not particularly concerned about short-term movements in share prices and are prepared to stick with companies they believe in through thick and thin. For this type of investor a short-term dip in a share price is seen as an opportunity to buy more shares at a bargain price, rather than as a selling signal. This investment approach is predicated on the belief that stock markets do tend to rise over long periods of time, making short-term volatility of little consequence.

Of course, the success of this approach depends on the quality of the companies invested in. Even large, blue-chip companies – considered to be relatively safe investments – are not immune to periods of poor performance. Marks & Spencer and Marconi spring to mind.

Traders adopt an entirely different approach, looking for short-term opportunities over weeks, days or even minutes. They ride the volatility of the stock markets like a surfer, looking to profit from the peaks and troughs through quick thinking and decisive action. They will use all information resources at their disposal – company news, broker analysis, directors' share dealings – looking for anything that could have a short-term effect on the share price. The idea is to be ahead of the game so that you are the first to react, anticipating the behaviour of other shareholders. Related to this is the 'science' of technical analysis – the study of share and stock market graphs or charts in the hope of predicting likely future movements. (We deal with this topic in Chapter 5).

Both approaches to investing have their advantages and disadvantages, and the internet is useful to both. But there is no guaranteed way to make money. Many investors will assign some of their capital to one strategy and some to the other. Just make sure that you know which is which and don't confuse the two. Lack of clarity on this point is a major reason why new investors lose money.

Summary of the advantages of investing online

- It's cheaper than other ways of investing.

- You get greater control over your investments and access to information twenty-four hours a day.

- Sophisticated research information is readily available.

2
Internet Basics

Introduction

The pace of technological change is breathtaking. No sooner have we bought the latest, fastest computer than another faster machine takes its place. It's enough to make us stop buying altogether in the hope that manufacturers eventually produce the ultimate machine, which will service all our needs in perpetuity. But that will never happen.

So if you haven't bought a computer yet, you'll just have to jump in there and get kitted out. Despite the marketing hype surrounding the very latest machines, you don't necessarily need to splash out on the best laptop or desktop to trade effectively online. Yes, it should be fast and capable of handling graphics, but plenty of mid-range computers do that perfectly well.

In this chapter we give you an overview of the basic tools you'll need to get started on investing online, plus tips on how to use the web safely and effectively.

Equipment

There are three main considerations when buying a PC: price, performance and service.

Price

You can buy a perfectly adequate internet-ready desktop computer for around £500 these days, as prices continue to fall in inverse proportion to their power. For £1000 and above you'll get the latest model with the fastest processor, a DVD-player and CD-rewriter as standard. But there's little point in going for a special deal that includes a scanner, web camera and so on if you are never likely to use these gadgets. Don't get carried away by marketing hype.

Performance

These days the incompatibility problems that bedevilled Apple Macintosh (Mac) computers and PCs using Microsoft Windows have largely disappeared. So the decision comes down to personal taste and appreciation of design. That said, you'll probably find life easier with a Windows PC, given that Microsoft hogs 90 per cent of the market. In November 2001 Microsoft launched its latest operating system, Windows XP, and most new PCs will probably come with this pre-loaded. But you don't necessarily need it and you may pick up a bargain as retailers sell off machines loaded with earlier versions such as Windows 98, 2000 and Millennium Edition (ME).

There are PCs now with superfast 2.0 Gigaherz (GHz) processors, but experts are increasingly questioning whether average users with standard requirements will need or notice such speed. Even PCs with 500 Megaherz (MHz) chips will cope with most modern demands. But whatever you do, don't stint on the Random Access Memory (RAM), as this helps you run several programs at once without the computer grinding to a halt. Go for 128 Megabytes (MB) minimum and 256 MB if you can.

It's also a good idea to go for a computer with a large screen that can handle multimedia applications. Investing online is heavy on the graphics, so you want to have clear, crisp images and to see as much information on one screen as you can. I would suggest fifteen inches as minimum, although you can go up to nineteen inches.

The hard drives of computers are enormous these days, mostly to cope with the huge video, photo and music files that people store on their systems. I get along happily with a 10 Gigabyte hard drive on my laptop, but then I'm not a computer games fanatic or a budding video director. New PCs are coming with 40 MB as standard, so data storage shouldn't be a problem.

Almost all PCs now come with a modem built in, so it's just a question of plugging your PC into the telephone socket to get online. The standard speed is now 56 kilobits per second. If you already have a computer that doesn't have an internal modem, buy an external one and plug it into the back of your computer. There are lots on the market for around £50, some offering fax and answering machine facilities too.

The latest laptops and notebooks also come with modems built in. Otherwise there is a whole range of credit-card-sized 'PCMCIA' modems on the market that simply slot in at the side of the computer. Some just enable you to connect to the internet via the normal telephone network; others also allow you to connect using your mobile phone, or link up to your company's computer system.

Software

It is a good idea to look closely at the software that comes bundled with a new PC, as this can often make hundreds of pounds' worth of difference when comparing prices of different makes and models. Think carefully about how you will use the computer and what software you are likely to need before buying.

Service

The quality of after-sales service is almost as important as the specification of the PC itself. If something does go wrong with your machine, the last thing you want is to have to send it back to the retailer or manufacturer. An 'on-site' warranty is best, where an engineer will come to your home and mend your PC for you. Most manufacturers' warranties last for just one year, although you can sometimes pay extra to extend the period.

Look closely at the quality of the telephone support offered. Home users are more likely to use PCs after work, so a helpline that shuts at 5 p.m. is not much use. Ideally, you want free, twenty-four-hour lifetime support.

Internet Service Providers (ISPs)

You need an ISP to act as your gateway to the internet. It handles the data flowing to and from your computer, including e-mail. There are hundreds to choose from and new PCs usually come with ISP software pre-loaded. You don't have to use these if you don't want to and there is nothing to stop you having several accounts. Sometimes ISPs break down and it is useful to have an alternative.

When choosing an ISP, check out the quality of the following features:

Technical support

Things can and do go wrong online and you need prompt and efficient help when they do. Look for an ISP with a helpline that stays open for as long as you stay up – twenty-four-hour, seven-days-a-week is ideal. But watch out for the cost – many ISPs charge 50p to £1 a minute for technical help. Some don't offer any help at all. Mac users should also make sure that technical help extends to them. In a Windows-dominated world, this isn't always the case.

Speed and reliability

Some ISPs have more reliable servers and sort out problems faster than others. You may have to pay a monthly fee for a higher level of reliability, but it could be worth the money. If you're engaged in some fast and furious share trading, the last thing you want is for your internet connection to break. Specialist internet magazines carry out exhaustive tests on all the leading ISPs, checking them for speed and reliability.

It is worth checking that your ISP is a member of the Internet

Service Providers Association. Its members follow a code of conduct that incorporates a standard complaints procedure should you be unhappy with your ISP's level of service. You can find a full list of ISPA members on its website (www.ispa.org.uk).

Telephone call charges

Even if your ISP service is free, you still have to pay connection charges. Telephone companies and ISPs offer a range of pricing packages to suit different types of user. If you don't use the internet much you might be better off with a 'pay-per-minute' package. But most online investors will profit from an unlimited-access deal for a fixed fee of £10 to £15 a month. This allows you to spend as long online as you like, whenever you like, without worrying about the size of the phone bill.

In practice, some services will automatically sever your connection after a few hours of continuous use to prevent the network from clogging up. This isn't usually a problem as you can reconnect straight away.

It can be a good idea to install a second telephone line just for internet use. If you are online a lot, a constant engaged tone will annoy people trying to ring you. Also, this allows you to talk to your ISP's technical support staff on the phone *and* connect to the internet at the same time. This can be very useful if you're trying to sort out problems, because you can test their suggested remedies without having to hang up.

The need for speed

If you are lucky enough to have access to high-speed 'broadband' services, these are ideal for serious investors. With these technologies digital data is fired into your PC ten times faster than via conventional modems. Also, the connection is always on, so there is no time wasted logging on and off to the network. The two rival versions in the retail market are ADSL (Asynchronous Digital Subscriber Line) from British Telecom and other telephone companies, and cable modems, supplied by the cable companies.

ADSL is a way of compacting digital data so that it can still be sent down the traditional copper telephone wires. Cable modems make use of the fibre optic network that cable companies have spent so long disrupting our roads to lay.

Unfortunately, the roll-out of these high-speed technologies has been dogged by delay, but they are undoubtedly the future. And believe me, once you've experienced a 512kbps connection you won't want to go back to your cranky old modem. Web pages load in a flash, programs are downloaded in seconds, rather than minutes, and video images are a lot smoother than the jerky fare we've been used to.

At the time of writing the pricing of these services was in flux, but after installation charges of around £100, you should expect to pay about £25 to £40 a month for high-speed internet access. Of course, telephone companies being what they are, there will be a whole raft of alternative tariffs incorporating various phone services. Within five years, though, I suspect most of the country will be on broadband and costs will have fallen sharply.

Security

Anti-virus software

This is an absolutely essential tool for any online investor. Although many viruses turn out to be hoaxes, malicious ones can still cause havoc on your computer. You should be particularly wary of e-mail attachments, as they are a favourite way of spreading executable programs known as 'Trojan Horses'. Once you've opened the file, the program automatically infiltrates your computer. One version sends the same message to all the contacts in your e-mail address book. Another more serious version can delete files on your hard drive.

But don't worry unduly. The latest anti-virus packages monitor your e-mail for you and spot attachments containing viruses. They will normally be able to repair or delete the infected file immediately. ISPs often perform systematic anti-virus checks on your e-mail before you even get it. All in all, you shouldn't become too concerned.

There are three main packages to choose from costing around £30:

Dr. Solomon's Home Guard   www.drsolomon.com
McAfee VirusScan (now part of Nework
    Associates)   www.nai.com
Norton AntiVirus   www.symantec.com

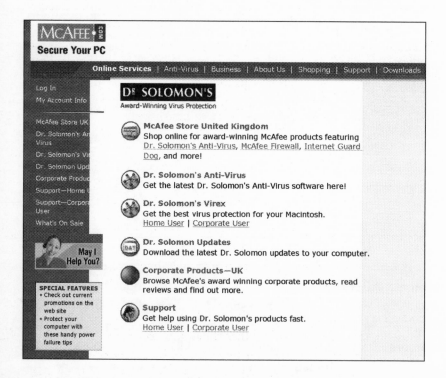

When you buy a new computer an anti-virus package will sometimes be included with the software bundle you get. Bear in mind that the program may have been sitting on the hard drive for several months after manufacture and will more than likely be out of date. Visit the software company's website and download the latest file containing all the known viruses, referred to as the signature file or the virus definition file. Your anti-virus package can detect which file version you have and tell you whether you need to download a new version. You normally receive a year's worth of updates after buying the software.

General safety tips

Fear over security continues to be a major drag on internet usage, especially when it comes to financial services. Hackers gaining access to trading accounts is a nightmare scenario that puts a lot of people off investing online. But most of these fears are unfounded.

All private and sensitive data is scrambled – encrypted – before it crosses the network. The standard level of encryption – 128-bit – is very strong and virtually impossible to crack. You can be confident that hackers will not be able to intercept and decode your details while they fly across the web in transit. Transacting online is actually a lot safer than dealing over the telephone.

But there is no room for complacency. You are responsible for keeping your passwords, user names and personal identification numbers safe from prying eyes. Be especially careful if you access your investment account at work on a shared computer. If you are called away from the desk before you have had time to log out, someone else could gain access to your account.

Here are some simple safety tips to help protect yourself when you are online:

- Never give your credit or debit card details over the net except via a secure server. You can tell that the link is secure when you see a closed padlock or unbroken key symbol at the bottom of your browser screen. The web address may also begin with https:// rather than the usual http://.

- Never write down or disclose passwords, log-in names or Personal Identification Numbers (PINs).

- Keep copies of e-mails to and from a company or service you use and print off copies of any agreements, contracts, application forms, or policy documents for safe keeping.

- Make sure you know what the company's privacy policy is and how it intends to keep your confidential data safe.

- Check that the company is properly authorised to conduct investment business. The Financial Services Authority, the regulator for the financial services industry, lists all authorised companies on a central register (www.thecentralregister.co.uk).

- If a website is offering a financial deal that looks too good to be true, it probably is. Steer clear. For news on the latest net frauds and scams try sites such as Internet Fraud Watch (www.fraud.org) and Internet Scambusters (www.scambusters.com).

- Be wary of giving too much credence to views expressed on investment bulletin boards, discussion groups and chat rooms. Unscrupulous people may be trying to manipulate markets in their favour. Also, never buy an investment solely on the basis of a tip from someone you don't know.

- If you have never used a particular website before, check it out thoroughly first. Look for contact address and telephone details, and try them out to check for authenticity. If you have any remaining doubts, don't deal with them.

- Look for sites that have been given a 'kitemark' certificate by an accreditation scheme, such as VeriSign, WebTrader, TRUSTe, trustUK, BBBOnLine, or JIPDEC. These schemes check out websites for authenticity, security and responsibility in the handling of personal data.

Navigating the Web

Browsers and how to use them effectively

A web browser is the free software program that helps you surf the net, loading web pages, storing website addresses and handling security. The two most popular programs are **Microsoft Internet Explorer** (IE) (<u>www.microsoft.com</u>) and **Netscape Navigator** (<u>www.netscape.com</u>), although there are others, such as **Opera** (<u>www.opera.com</u>).

There is nothing to stop you having a number of browsers on your system – you don't have to stick with the browser your ISP has given you. CD-ROMS accompanying computer and internet magazines often contain the latest versions of the various browsers available. You can load them on to your computer and try them out to see which you prefer. It is far quicker to load software this way – downloading browsers from the net can take hours. Both the popular browsers perform much the same functions, so it comes down to personal preference as to which one you use.

It is important to keep your browser software up to date as the designers are constantly releasing new versions with enhanced features. The latest versions will notify you automatically when this happens, so all you have to do is click on a link, go to the website and begin downloading.

Here is a round-up of the most useful browser functions:

OPENING SEVERAL BROWSER WINDOWS

Online investors often need to have access to several sources of information at the same time. For example, you might want to read financial news on one website, look at broker analysis of a particular company on another and have your trading account open ready to put your researches into practice. You can have all this information on one screen by opening new browser windows and loading the various websites into each window.

In the latest versions of both leading browsers you do this by clicking on the 'File' tab at the top of the browser, selecting 'New' and then 'Window' or 'Navigator Window'. Alternatively, each time you click on the browser icon on your desktop screen or toolbar, a new browser window opens up. You can either switch quickly between the websites by clicking on the tabs at the bottom of the screen, or resize and move the browser windows to make them all fit on your screen.

REFRESHING OR RELOADING PAGES

Financial data, such as share prices, are constantly changing. If your web page doesn't refresh itself automatically, or you don't have access to live streaming information, you'll have to click on the 'Refresh' or 'Reload' button in the browser menu bar every now and then to make sure you have the latest information.

PRINTING WEB PAGES

You can print off pages from the web easily by clicking on the 'Print' button in the browser menu bar. This is useful for printing off contract notes confirming an online share deal you've just made.

SAVING PAGES

You don't have to stay online all the time while researching new investment opportunities. Either save the web page in its entirety or highlight the text you want to copy and paste it into a new word document for reading later. The latest browser versions let you save pages in a number of ways. For example, you can exclude all the graphics if you like and just save the text.

BOOKMARKING WEBSITES

Bookmarking is the best thing your web browser can do. Instead of having to remember web addresses and type them into the browser's address box each time, you can store them for easy access later. With

Netscape Navigator, you click on the 'Bookmarks' pull-down menu and click the 'Add Bookmark' option. With Microsoft's Internet Explorer you click on the 'Favorites' pull-down menu and then click on 'Add To Favorites'. You can also click on the right mouse button while pointing at the page and you'll be offered the same options. Or you can just hold down the 'Control' button and press 'D' on your keyboard and it will bookmark the page in both browsers.

Bear in mind that when you do this you will bookmark the precise page you're on. So if you like the site as a whole, and not just the specific page you happen to be looking at, go back to the **home page** first before bookmarking.

It is a good idea to organise your bookmarks into subject folders so you can find them easily. In Internet Explorer you choose **Organize Favorites** from the **Favorites** menu. In Netscape you can choose **Communicator, Bookmarks, Edit Bookmarks** or, more directly, click on the dedicated **Bookmarks** tab and then choose **Edit Bookmarks**. When you tell your browser to bookmark a page, it will often give the file a very long title, but you can change this to whatever you want.

To return to a favourite site click on the 'Bookmarks' or 'Favorites' tab located in your browser's menu bar and select the relevant website address from the pull-down list. If you're online, you'll go straight to that web page. It is good practice to save your Bookmarks folder to disk as it is a valuable resource.

Using search engines and directories

Looking for specific information on the web can be frustrating if you don't take the time to learn some basic search techniques. Search engines and directories can be pretty blunt instruments and wading through pages and pages of irrelevant material is very frustrating. They are gradually getting better as many directories have developed UK-specific sites now, but here are some tips to help you pinpoint the information you are after:

• Try to use unique words and phrases in the search box.

- Make sure you spell the words correctly.

- Use several words rather than just a couple to help narrow down the field.

- Learn how the search engine handles upper and lower case.

- Use 'Boolean operators' where relevant – words such as 'AND', 'NOT', 'NEAR' – or the search engine's own version.

- Compare results from several search engines or use a meta-search engine which trawls through lots of other engines and directories.

- Try other sources of information within search engines, such as Usenet newsgroups, as well as the web.

- When you're browsing all the 'hits' thrown up by a search, open new browser windows when clicking on the ones you're most interested in rather than reading each entry one by one and then pressing the back button to the results page. You'll save a lot of time this way.

SOME USEFUL SEARCH SITES

My favourite search engines are Copernic (www.copernic.com) and Google (www.google.co.uk). Copernic trawls through lots of other

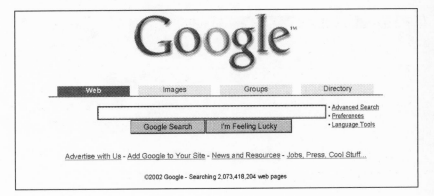

search engines, directories, Usenet lists (see below) and e-mail databases looking for what you want. This takes longer but the search is obviously more comprehensive. Google is lightning fast and excellent for quick searches.

Below is a list of other leading search engines, directories and other online research resources for your list of Bookmarks:-

AltaVista UK	www.uk.altavista.com
Excite UK	www.excite.co.uk
Go	www.go.com
Lycos	www.lycos.co.uk
Mirago	www.mirago.co.uk
Northern Light	www.northernlight.com
WebCrawler	http://webcrawler.com
NBCi	www.nbci.com
Britannica	www.britannica.com
Yahoo! UK	http://uk.yahoo.com

About.com   www.about.com
DMOZ Open Directory Project   http://dmoz.org

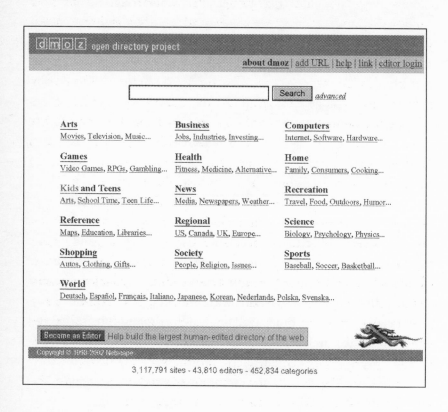

The Argus Clearinghouse   www.clearinghouse.internet
Galaxy   www.galaxy.com
Magellan   http://magellan.excite.com
EuroSeek   www.euroseek.com
LookSmart   www.looksmart.com
UKOnline   www.ukonline.com
All4One   www.all4one.com
MetaCrawler   http://metacrawler.com
Dogpile   www.dogpile.com
Ask Jeeves   www.ask.co.uk
Powersearch   www.powersearch.com

Usenet newsgroups

Usenet is the collective name for the thousands of subject-specific discussion groups and newsgroups on the internet. It can be a valuable resource and a place to swap ideas, news and tips. When you download 'news' on the net, it doesn't mean news in the conventional sense, but the messages left by people. These messages are often called 'articles' too, just to confuse matters. These days they can also include photographs, video, animation and sound.

Usenet shouldn't be confused with bulletin boards or chat rooms. Bulletin boards tend to be places where people can swap messages on particular websites and chat rooms are 'real-time' environments where people can swap instantaneous messages.

There are two main ways of accessing Usenet. The first is to use your news reader program included with the latest versions of web browsers. Instead of accessing the web, you go to your internet service provider's 'news server' – a computer that deals exclusively with Usenet. You can browse all the groups and carry out detailed subject searches this way, choosing to subscribe to any groups you find interesting. You can also access all these newsgroups through the web by going to sites such as Google Groups (http://groups.google.com) – formerly called Deja.com.

You can either enter a more specific search term or browse the newsgroup subject titles looking for relevant groups.

TIPS ON POSTING MESSAGES

Discussion topics are called 'threads' and you can simply reply to views already expressed or start a new thread if you like. People who post messages – 'posters' – may include their e-mail addresses so that you can contact them direct if you want. Don't give out your e-mail address as a matter of course, though, or you might become the target of unwanted e-mails, known as 'spam'.

You can start a new message within your newsreader program by clicking on 'New Message' in the menu bar, or via a Usenet search engine, such as Google Groups mentioned above. To start a new message just click on the 'New Message' tabs in your newsreader menu bar.

Before posting messages make sure you know a little about the Usenet etiquette. Read the Frequently Asked Questions (FAQ) file in the newsgroup, if there is one, and look around for any other 'Help' files to get you started. You can make yourself very unpopular if you waste people's time with irrelevant messages or annoying habits, such as typing in capitals – known as 'shouting'.

General news resources

Good investors will keep abreast of world events and politics as well as financial news. In an increasingly global economy, events in one part of the world have a knock-on effect in another. Keeping an eye on the big picture can help you make better investment decisions.

There is a wealth of news on the web, most of it free, and you can also subscribe to various journals and magazines. Several newspapers provide comprehensive archive facilities allowing you to look for stories that are months or even years old. This is a considerable advantage over the traditional newspaper. Online news resources give you video and radio, as well as written articles.

Here is a round-up of useful news resources:

NATIONAL NEWSPAPERS

Sunday Times	www.sunday-times.co.uk
The Times	www.the-times.co.uk
Financial Times	www.ft.com
Telegraph	www.telegraph.co.uk
Guardian	www.guardian.co.uk
Independent	www.independent.co.uk
Daily Mail	www.dailymail.co.uk
Mirror	www.mirror.co.uk
Daily Express	www.express.co.uk
Evening Standard	www.thisislondon.co.uk

MAGAZINES

Economist	www.economist.com
New Statesman	www.newstatesman.co.uk

Spectator   www.spectator.co.uk
New Scientist   www.newscientist.co.uk

NEWS BROADCASTERS
BBC   www.bbc.co.uk

ITN	www.itn.co.uk
PA Newswire	www.pa.press.internet
Reuters	www.reuters.com
CNN	www.cnn.com

NEWS AGGREGATORS

BBC Monitoring	www.monitor.bbc.co.uk
NewsNow	www.newsnow.co.uk
Newswatch-UK	www.newswatch.co.uk
NewsHub	www.newshub.com

TECHNOLOGY NEWS

Wired	www.wired.com
Internet.com	www.internet.com
Net Imperative	www.netimperative.co.uk
NUA Surveys	www.nua.ie

Useful programs or 'plug-ins'

Surfing the web is now a rich multimedia experience incorporating sound, images, video and animation. And this is true as much for investors as other types of web user. To make the most of all that the web can offer you, you need the right software that will let you watch corporate mini-videos, for example, or listen to financial news on internet radio. These software programs are called 'plug-ins', despite the fact that they don't actually plug in.

Software companies are competing madly with each other to make their versions of these plug-ins the definitive version. There are no standards, so that if a video file, say, is in a format devised by one particular software company, you have to download the plug-in that can read those files. Video files in another format will require another plug-in. There are usually several programs available that do much the same thing. This can be confusing, but at least it gives you the opportunity to try out a few and see which one you like best.

The latest browsers have several essential plug-ins already built in, but you don't have to stick with these. You can download alternative programs from the software companies' websites. A popular program for music and video, and the one that seems to be dominating the market, is **RealPlayer** (www.real.com). Microsoft has its own version called **Windows Media Player** (www.microsoft.com) incorporated into Internet Explorer. Apple's version is called **QuickTime** (www.apple.com/quicktime).

Another important program is **Macromedia Shockwave Player** (www.shockwave.com). This enables your browser to handle animated graphics and other advanced website design features. A lot of websites are using this program these days, so if you don't have it, your browser won't be able to load the page properly. Usually, if this happens, the website provides a link to the software company so that you can download the required software there and then. The quickest way to load these programs on your system is to log on to the internet early in the morning (when most Americans are still in bed), or look out for free CD-ROMS accompanying internet and PC magazines. These often have lots of useful plug-ins on them and it

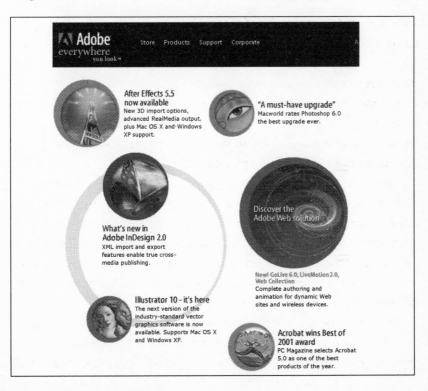

takes a fraction of the time loading them on to your hard drive.

A lot of documents on the internet are now designed using **Adobe Acrobat** (www.adobe.com), which helps make pages look exactly as they would in a conventional book or magazine. But you need the **Acrobat Reader** plug-in to read these files (called 'PDF files'). It is well worth getting, especially if you plan to print off documents – the quality is excellent. Also, websites often have forms that you need to fill in. Rather than completing them online, you can print them off before posting.

3
Getting Started

Introduction

Investing using the internet has been one of the most dynamic and exciting areas of financial services over the last few years. For the first time in history private investors have had many of the resources available to professional investors in the City. If information is power, private investors have been at a considerable disadvantage for far too long.

Now there are hundreds of investment-related websites catering for all types of investor and covering every subject. Research and analysis that was once solely for professionals is available online for all, often for free. Even major international stockbrokers that would normally charge their institutional clients large sums for company research and investment recommendations are publishing their views online.

Soon, investment information – the raw data that underpin investment decisions – will become as ordinary as baked beans. We will be able to find almost anything we want online whenever we want it. But having access to facts and figures is only half the story. Knowing how to interpret those figures and how to act on them is the difficult part. The internet is a very sophisticated tool, but it is still just a tool. It can't make you wealthy by itself. Of course, there is no end of opinion and general advice online, too, but by and large, online investors are left to make their own decisions. This can be daunting, especially for new investors.

So in this chapter we look at useful websites for beginners to investing. We show you how you can set up 'fantasy portfolios' of shares that you can watch and study while you learn the ropes and gain confidence in your own abilities. We show you how to shop around for an online broker, how to set up an account, and how investing online works.

Get Educated!

As most online brokers are execution-only, novice investors need to do their homework first before plunging into the exciting world of online investment. In the US they are far more knowledgeable about investing and finance in general because they have a much longer history of self-sufficiency. They had no Welfare State to rely on for pension provision so had to learn how to build wealth for the future.

In this country we still largely cling to cash savings accounts and maybe the odd Personal Equity Plan or Individual Savings Account. The majority of the 12 million or so shareholders in this country actually have just one or two shares, which they tend to sit on and forget about. Investing online is all about taking control of your finances, getting familiar with research techniques and building confidence to make your own investment decisions. This can take as much or as little work as you like, depending on whether you want to be a 'steady-as-she-goes' long-term investor, or a day-trading dynamo out to make a million in a flash.

Basic investment jargon explained

Company reports and accounts can be daunting things – there are so many facts, figures and jargon words. But the following is a selection of the important elements you need to look at to assess whether a company is in good shape:

Profits – ideally, you want to see pre-tax profits rising strongly compared with previous years.

Cash Flow – the main reason why companies go bust is because they run out of cash. A company may be owed a lot of money and include this in its profit statement, but if it's not in the bank yet, there may be cause for concern.

Balance sheet – this summarises everything the company owns and owes on the date the accounts are drawn up. It can be the most accurate picture of a company's overall health.

Gearing – this tells you how much the company has borrowed in relation to the amount of shareholders' funds (equity) in the business. If a company is 'highly geared' the interest payments on its borrowings will be high. This isn't a problem if the company is doing well and growing. In fact, high borrowing may well help it to expand more quickly. But if things aren't going so well, the company may not be able to repay the interest and the creditors may well call in the loans, forcing the company to fold.

Earnings per share (eps) – this is an important ratio for showing how much profit after tax and other deductions (net profit) is actually being earned per share. You simply divide the net profit by the number of shares in issue. It is usually expressed as X pence per share. Looking at whether the eps is rising or falling over time is one of the most important indicators of whether a company is really making money for its shareholders.

Dividend per share – this is simply the amount the company has agreed to pay from its profits to shareholders divided by the number of shares in issue.

There are many more performance indicators and complicated accounting figures than the ones mentioned, but these are the most important for new investors to get to grips with. Even these are difficult enough!

AND WHAT ABOUT ALL THESE ABBREVIATIONS IN THE FINANCIAL PAGES?

In papers such as the *Financial Times* and some other broadsheet newspapers (and, increasingly, on financial websites), all the companies publicly quoted on the stock market are listed along with their current share prices. But there are other important financial indicators too. These are designed to help investors compare one company with another and assess whether they are getting value for money. Below are some of the columns you'll find in the *FT*'s London Share Service pages. Let's go through each of the columns step by step, but bear in mind that the columns can change depending on the day of the week.

(Col.1) Company Name   Self-explanatory.

(Col.2) Notes   Each newspaper may have its own symbols. In the *FT*, for example, a ♣ symbol means that you can get a free interim/annual report from the company.

(Col.3) Price   Share prices are usually expressed in pence. The figure quoted is actually the mid-price between the buying and selling price at the end of the trading day (4.30 p.m. for the London Stock Exchange). If you wanted to buy a share you would pay a higher price than you would get if you wanted to sell them. The difference between these two prices is called the **bid-offer spread**. The wider the spread, the more profit goes to the market maker. The letters 'xd' after the price mean 'ex dividend' which tells you that if you bought the shares now you would be too late to benefit from the dividend for the half or full year.

(Col.4) + or –   This tells you how many pence the share price moved up or down compared with the previous day's closing share price. On a Monday in the *FT* you usually see a column headed 'W'k % ch'nge'. This tells you how much the share price has changed up or down over the week, expressed as a percentage of the share price at the beginning of the week.

(Cols 5 & 6) 52-week high/low   These columns tell you the highest and lowest prices the shares have reached over a rolling 52-week period. It gives you a good indication of how the share price is performing currently relative to its previous performance.

(Col.7) Volume 000s   This tells you how many thousands of the company's shares were bought and sold in the market yesterday.

(Col.8) Yield   This is the dividend income per share expressed as a percentage of the share price. If you're looking for maximum income from your investments you might look at shares with high yield figures. But a high yield can also indicate that the company isn't growing very fast or is quite risky. As the level of dividend is arbitrarily decided by the directors of the company and approved by shareholders, it isn't a very accurate indication by itself of a company's overall worth or value for money.

(Col.9) P/E

The **price/earnings ratio** is a better indicator, especially for gauging whether a company's share price is cheap or expensive compared with similar companies in the same sector. You get the P/E by dividing the share price by the earnings per share (eps) figure. Investors are prepared to pay more for shares whose earnings they think are going to rise strongly, so demand pushes the share price up. This in turn will give the company a high P/E ratio. A high P/E can indicate a high-growth company, but it can also indicate that the company's earnings have taken a sudden, maybe temporary, hit. Generally the P/E ratio is seen as a kind of barometer of confidence in a company's prospects.

On Monday in the *FT* you usually see these abbreviations in place of some of the other columns:

Div net	This tells you the net (after-tax) dividend per share.
Div cov	Dividend cover is broadly the number of times the agreed dividend could have been paid out from net profits. It is a good indicator of the company's ability to pay the dividend and also its level of generosity.
Mkt cap£m	Short for **market capitalisation**. This is a measure of the company's worth on the stock market. It is simply the current share price multiplied by the total number of shares in issue. On the stock market, companies can have market valuations ranging from just a few million pounds to over a hundred billion pounds.

Investment websites for beginners

The following websites are my favourites for providing an easy-to-understand introduction to investing:

THIS IS MONEY – www.thisismoney.com

This is a friendly, approachable personal finance site produced by the owners of the *Daily Mail*, *Mail on Sunday* and *Evening Standard* newspapers. It is editorial in approach with the emphasis on news and general guides to educate and inform investors. There is plenty

7 January 2002

of help with choosing ISAs and unit trusts, for example, plus a cheap share-dealing service (£15 per deal) thanks to a tie-up with StockAcademy, the online stockbroker.

MOTLEY FOOL UK – www.fool.co.uk

The Motley Fool is a US concept successfully imported into the UK. It is known for its irreverent and fun approach to the whole business of investment, symbolised by its court jester logo. Registered members may be called 'Fools', but the site isn't frivolous. The approach is designed to woo novice investors and lead them gently into the world of investing without overwhelming them with unintelligible jargon. There's plenty of valuable information on how to plan for the future, how to choose a broker (including a comparison table of some of the cheapest brokers around), plus guides and tips on different trading and investing strategies.

The site also has a well-managed 'Discussion Boards' section, where members chat to each other on various topics, not necessarily investment-related. Listening to the views of more experienced investors is a good way to learn the ropes. But avoid acting on such opinions alone. Unless you do your own research, you're just gambling, really. And as we know, most gamblers lose in the long run.

The site also includes sections on other areas of finance, such as insurance and pensions, with comparison tools to help you find the best financial products. It is also worth having a look at its US counterpart – www.fool.com – for news and comment from across the Pond.

FTINVESTOR – www.ft.com/investor

This dedicated investment site from the *Financial Times* newspaper is an excellent resource for company news and stock market data from around the world. There are share tips, commentaries and analysis that may be a little daunting for the novice investor at first, but it is still definitely a site to bookmark. Registered users can sign up for twice-daily newsletters by e-mail as well, so that you are kept bang up to date.

In fact, all the *Financial Times* sites are worth bookmarking. This includes the newspaper's main site – <u>www.ft.com</u> – and its personal-finance site, *FT* Your Money – <u>www.ftyourmoney.com</u>. The sites rightly strengthen the *FT*'s reputation as one of the world's leading providers of business and financial data. The breadth and quality of information available is extremely impressive.

INVESTORS CHRONICLE – <u>www.investorschronicle.co.uk</u>

Investors Chronicle is yet another of the *FT*'s suite of business and finance publications. It is sold in shops as a magazine, but also has a very useful website. Considered by many to be the private investor's bible, *IC* has covered investment-related topics for many, many years. In fact, it can trace its roots back to 1860! It aims to cover every company listed on the London Stock Exchange. Investors who register for the free site have access to news and analysis, plus tools to help them find a suitable broker and the best-performing investment funds. If you want access to *IC*'s share tips and broker recommendations, however, you have to wield the plastic – a year's subscription costs £125. The tips are backed up by expert research and there's bags of advice and guidance on a wide range of subjects.

AMPLE INTERACTIVE INVESTOR – <u>www.ample.com</u>

Interactive Investor International was one of the first companies into

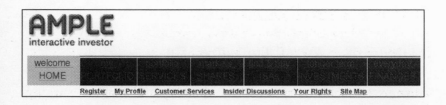

this market, a pioneer in the provision of high-quality investment information to the private investor. After a period of rapid growth and success culminating in a stock market flotation, it has since had a rocky ride, thanks to the general stock market malaise and the trouncing of internet-related stocks in particular. It has now been taken over by Ample, the online investment arm of Australian bank AMP.

'Triple I', as it was commonly known, expanded aggressively to become a general personal-finance portal, with links to product providers as well as guides and financial news. It was one of the first sites to introduce portfolio tracking, enabling investors to keep tabs on their investments, whether real or imaginary. You can see how much you're worth and how much profit you've made, and look at company share price graphs.

Share prices are delayed by fifteen minutes. If you want real-time prices you have to pay for them. III's 'Desktop Trader' product provides real-time streaming prices, news, analysis and research, for £15 (plus VAT) a month. You can see exactly what you are worth that second and act on news and company announcements straight away. Novice investors may not need this immediately, but it is worth noting.

The site also has plenty of general guides and guest writers commenting on various aspects of investment. It is an excellent educational resource supplemented by a fairly busy investor bulletin board, where novices and experienced traders swap views on all kinds of topics. Of course, as the site is under new management, the flavour and approach may change. Ample is primarily an online investment funds retailer, so we can expect more emphasis on funds in the coming year.

CITYWIRE – www.citywire.co.uk

In the past a lot of investment news websites provided just that – investment news. There was no attempt to analyse it or explain the jargon. They were intimidating for novice investors. Citywire attempts to make more sense of company and market news by providing analysis from a team of journalists, many of whom are now qualified to give specific investment advice. It is a neat, well-focused site providing relevant news in bite-size packages. It also provides company data and news of secret share purchases, sales by company directors and other influential shareholders.

One particularly interesting feature is a service called 'Funds Insider'. Many investors follow particular fund managers, withdrawing their investments if their favourite whizz-kids jump ship to another company. Citywire enables investors to track the performance of individual managers, no matter which fund management company they work for. You simply choose a fund sector – UK All Companies or Europe Smaller Companies, say – then a time period (up to three years), and Citywire ranks the best managers, giving them an average personal monthly performance rate. You can see how they compare against the sector average. Click on the fund of a particular manager and you can see how the fund has performed and read related news stories.

Citywire may not offer flashy design, but its straightforward approach, focused on providing practical information and advice for investors, is well worth having in your armoury of useful websites.

HEMMINGTON SCOTT – www.hemscott.net

Hemmington Scott has transformed itself from a rather dowdy publisher into one of the leading online financial information providers for businesses and private investors alike. Its new service, Hemscott.net, is both an Internet Service Provider and information resource offering free and subscription services. It was voted 'Best Research Provider' in the 2001 *Investors Chronicle* UK Investment Awards and deservedly so. Once you've registered with the site there are a number of free services available to you, including e-mail news alerts on your chosen companies, archived news, details of directors' share dealings, as well as the usual share price and portfolio tracking services.

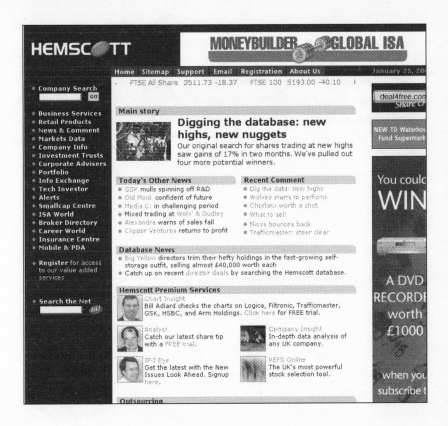

More investors may be prepared to pay for sophisticated analytical tools, such as Company REFS – extremely detailed statistics covering every aspect of a company's finances. It isn't cheap, though: £62 a month or a one-off charge of £675. You can try it out free for fourteen days. Other subscription services include *Hemscott Analyst* – share tips backed up fundamental company research – for £10 a month or £99 for a full year's subscription.

Hemscott cleverly appeals to all levels of investor through its provision of basic free and in-depth paid-for services. It is a very powerful and well-designed resource that should be the home page for many novice investors.

YAHOO! FINANCE – http://uk.finance.yahoo.com

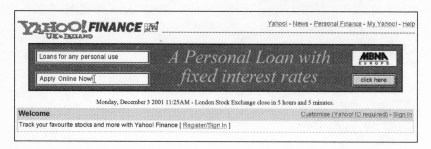

The world's largest search portal has fingers in most pies these days and investing is no exception. Its dedicated UK and Ireland site is a cornucopia of useful links to investment-related websites, several of which are described here. It doesn't have much of its own content, but provides a useful jumping-off point for investors, collating guides, tips, prices and news from a whole range of sources. There are lively bulletin boards to swap views with fellow investors, too.

ADVFN (ADVANCED FINANCIAL NETWORK) – www.advfn.com

This is a very busy investment site that could appear overwhelming for the novice investor. But I've included it in this section because it has very lively bulletin boards (BBs) that are at times informative, annoying, abusive and erudite. All human life is there! Investors will quickly get a feel for different investment approaches as self-styled investment gurus exchange punches in the safe confines of the internet, where anonymity is preserved thanks to the convention of using nicknames. There is a 'Premium BB' as well for serious investors who don't like to mix it with the rabble. This costs £5 (plus VAT) a month, but for this you also get live share prices and a host of other services to help you choose your investments and monitor them.

Once you've registered there are lots of free services available, such as portfolio tracking, share prices and fundamental company data (profits, turnover and so on). Subscription services have tiered pricing structures rising to £99.99 (plus VAT) a month for its 'Platinum' level. With this you receive live streaming Level II data, which is what the professional investors in the City have access to. You can see what the market makers – the companies that set the buy and sell prices for shares throughout the day – are up to.

ADVFN is not the prettiest site but it is comprehensive and a useful addition to the research armoury of the online investor. It also incorporates UK-iNvest, the investment information site previously owned by GlobalNet Financial.

MX MONEYEXTRA – www.moneyextra.com

The world of online financial services is in constant flux it seems. First, there was a personal finance website called Moneyworld. This was subsumed into another personal finance website called MX Moneyextra. MX Moneyextra has now merged with a firm of independent financial advisers called Willis National. The result is MX Moneyextra. How long it stays this way is anyone's guess. The investment section of the site has enjoyed an upgrade recently and it makes a welcome change. Once you've registered to join the 'Moneyextra Club' you can track your portfolio – including shares in overseas markets – apply for free company annual reports and receive investment newsletters.

The site isn't top-heavy on the research side, but this at least makes it seem more accessible for the new investor. In fact, the investment sections of the personal finance websites are more skilled at presenting information in an accessible and less intimidating way generally. There are discussion bulletin boards, special offers and a fun, clubby atmosphere.

SHARECAST – www.sharecast.com

This is a neat, simple site specialising in providing company news stories and collating press comment to help investors with their research. You can use the site's archive search engine to find a particular piece of news or comment as well, and there is also basic market news and information.

LONDON STOCK EXCHANGE –
www.londonstockexchange.com

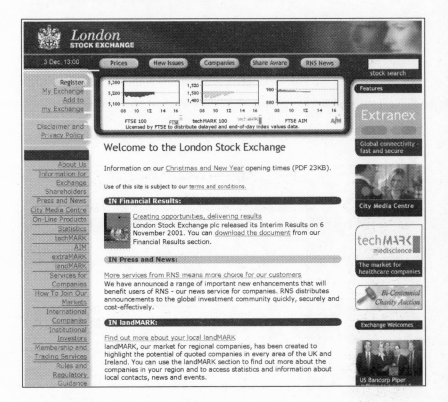

The LSE's official site contains lots of useful background information for private investors, as well as share prices and details of the companies listed in the technology sector techMARK. There's information on the Alternative Investment Market – the smaller, less tightly regulated market for fledgling companies – and simple guides and glossaries.

TRUSTNET – www.trustnet.com

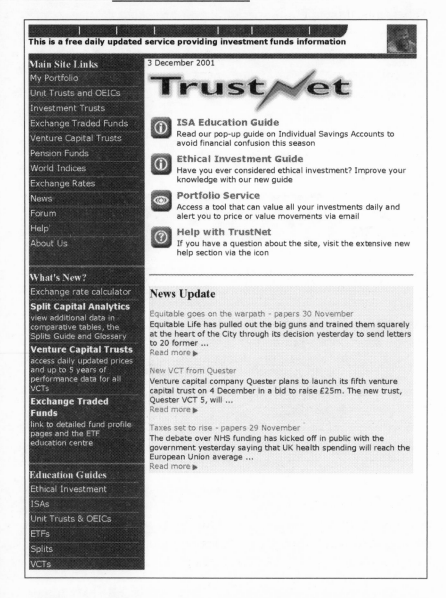

TrustNet started off as a site tightly focused on UK investment trusts, providing price, performance and portfolio data for each trust. It has since expanded the service to include all investment funds, including unit trusts and open-ended investment companies (OEICS). It is a superbly detailed site, telling you everything you need to know about the management, investment strategy and main investments of most funds.

Teletext – www.teletext.co.uk

The website of the famous TV information service provides investment news and live share prices on a stock-by-stock basis.

UK Online Investing – www.ukonlineinvesting.com

This is a relatively simple site designed for 'high-net-worth individuals' and 'sophisticated investors' – or so it says. In fact, the site offers a useful investment newsletter containing company news, research and analysis. Just type in your e-mail address to subscribe and away you go.

Setting up a portfolio manager

Most of the sites reviewed above allow you to set up a portfolio of shares and other investments that you can then monitor. Such 'stockwatch' or 'portfolio manager' services are a useful way of encouraging you to come back to that particular site, rather than the scores of other investment information sites that seem to be springing up everywhere. They are useful for investors who may want to monitor their existing investments without necessarily setting up a brokerage account and buying any more. You can get an up-to-date snapshot of your wealth (or lack of it) whenever you like.

Setting up a 'fantasy portfolio' – investments that you don't own but might like to own – is useful for testing your investment theories. Will you make paper profits or paper losses? How good has your research been? And what would you do in real life if one of your shares suddenly fell by 10 per cent?

I would strongly recommend that novice investors get to know the investment ropes first, before committing real money to this potentially hazardous activity. It is so easy to set up an online brokerage account these days – just ten minutes in some cases – that you can be buying and selling like a day-trading dervish before you understand the first thing about investment. This is a sure-fire way of losing all your capital fast.

Fantasy portfolios give you the opportunity to learn how to select stocks, research them and monitor them. With most portfolio managers you can click on links to find out related news stories and to plot graphs showing share price performance over a period of your choice. These graphing tools are getting very sophisticated now, enabling you to compare your chosen stock against market indices or other stocks in the same sector.

Watching and waiting is frequently the best strategy the online investor can adopt. Share prices can often follow recognisable patterns of behaviour. Watching these patters over a few weeks or months can give new investors a better feel for the way markets behave. For example, a common mistake investors make is to buy when a share price has already risen sharply and to sell when it has already fallen sharply. Share prices rarely rise in smooth, continuous straight lines – there are fluctuations. So it is better to wait until investors decide to take some profit after a sustained price rise before buying. The price will drop back a little before resuming its movement upwards (provided, of course, that the company is still making profits and growing as fast as predicted).

Running a fantasy portfolio is a great way of building confidence in your own decision-making abilities. It is all very well selecting stocks. The tricky part is knowing what to do with them. When do you take profits? When do you cut your losses and move on? While you are pondering these great investment conundrums you can be getting to grips with the jargon, reading the views of others in newsletters and bulletin boards, and learning how to interpret the many and various financial indicators that tell us how a company is performing and likely to perform in the future.

Even the most well-funded solidly growing companies can be buffeted by world events, such as economic recessions, wars, major lawsuits. Investors have to learn the difference between a share price drop caused by general pessimism about the state of the markets and a drop caused by something fundamentally wrong with the company.

We will discuss all the different investment strategies, performance indicators and analytical tools available to the online investor in Chapter 6.

Investment Clubs

Setting up or joining an investment club is an excellent way to learn about investing in a safe, cheap and fun environment. A group of friends or work colleagues (up to twenty, usually) get together and contribute regularly to a fund that is used to buy shares or other investments. There is no set contribution level, although £20 or £25 a month is common.

The idea has proved immensely popular – there are now over 11,000 investment clubs in the UK, from firemen to nurses, all clubbing together to buy shares. In 1999 there were just 3800, so the rate of growth has been remarkable. Some clubs have done so well they've even beaten the professional investors in the City at their own game.

According to ProShare, 86 per cent of club members now use the internet for research and dealing. Most brokers have cottoned on to the popularity of investment clubs and offer trading accounts specifically designed for them. Dealing commissions are often cheaper than for individual investors.

What makes investment clubs so useful is that they are a safe place to learn, as members can share their experiences. It is also an effective way of spreading risk. If some of your investments take a nosedive, the losses are split between you. The profits are split too, but while you're learning, it's better to be safe than sorry. For more information on how to set up and run an investment club, go to the ProShare website (www.proshare.org.uk).

ProShare is an industry-funded body that promotes wider share ownership. It produces a helpful starter pack (£29.50) for investment clubs, which includes all the forms you need to fill in, plus advice on how to organise your club, find a broker and keep account of the money. You can order it online or over the phone (020 7220 1730).

Once you've bought your pack, membership of ProShare Investment Clubs is free for the first year. This is what you get:

- *Dividend* magazine for each club member: investment club news, views and tips.

- A free copy of the latest issue of REFS (Really Essential Financial Statistics) worth £65. It gives you detailed financial data on every London Stock Exchange company.

- The facility to set up your own investment club website and e-mail through ProShare's own internet service. You also receive portfolio management software.

- Access to ProShare's Investment Club Helpline for advice on how to run your club.

- Free entry to newspaper-backed investment club competitions to find the best-performing clubs.

- Discounts on investment seminars.

In the next chapter we tackle the subject of online stockbrokers – how to choose the best one to suit your investment style and your budget.

CHAPTER 4

Online Stockbrokers

Introduction

It hasn't been the best time for online stockbrokers recently. Fierce price competition has forced dealing commissions down considerably as more and more brokers have entered an already crowded market. To run a discount brokerage business you need high transaction volumes to compensate for the fact that your profit margins are wafer thin. Unfortunately, those volumes have been far lower than expected owing to the fears of US recession, the bursting of the dot.com bubble and the uncertainty following the terrorist attacks on 11 September 2001.

Consequently it has been a struggle for many brokers, particularly the foreign newcomers who have been trying to establish themselves in this market. I confidently predict that by the time this book is published a few of the companies mentioned here will have merged with others or have been closed down completely. Being owned by a rich parent company is no guarantee of success either. In November 2001 Crédit Suisse First Boston, the major US investment house, sold its UK brokerage – DLJDirect – to T.D. Waterhouse, the Canadian-owned internet broker, after disappointment at the rate of growth in this country.

Sharepeople, a UK internet broker, was taken over by American Express in January 2001. Consors, the German-owned broker, won a temporary reprieve from its banking parent, after it had shown disappointing take-up figures. Doubts over StockAcademy's future must remain, after one of its two shareholders, GlobalNet Financial, was forced to sell its investment information site, UK-iNvest, in 2001. And so it goes on.

But what does all this mean for the online investor? Uncertainty for one thing – and investors hate uncertainty. It can also be quite annoying to choose a broker, set up an account, learn how to use the site's resources, only for the entire approach, design and, perhaps, pricing structure, to change following an acquisition. The inconvenience of setting up an account with a broker that then has to close is far greater.

Ironically, it is the traditional brokers, whose internet dealing services are relatively recent, that are probably in the best position to ride out the tough times. They have an established clientele, most of whom pay for advice through higher dealing commissions on telephone orders. Internet dealing is not their major revenue source.

The situation is far more serious for the execution-only brokers as they can't charge more for advice. They just have to hope that their US and European backers are in it for the long term and are not tempted to pull the plug. The number of online investors is steadily increasing, albeit at a slower rate than predicted, and stock markets are resilient, bouncing back time after time in the face of world events. So the future is still bright for those brokers with deep pockets and the confidence to be innovative and responsive to their customers' needs.

More resources, more choice

Since the UK online investing phenomenon took root in 1997, the breadth and quality of services has improved dramatically for investors. Not only has the technology itself become faster and more reliable, but the range of services has improved too. To start with, we could invest in UK shares and that was it. Now a growing number of brokers are offering access to international markets, giving investors the welcome opportunity to broaden their horizons and buy shares in foreign companies.

Not only that, but the range of investment classes has increased as well. Now you can buy investment funds online via a broker, fund supermarket or intermediary. You can manage all your investments online in a tax-efficient self-select Individual Savings Account (ISA). Pensions are moving online too, with the introduction of the no-frills stakeholder pension and do-it-yourself self-invested personal pensions (SIPPs). You can also buy futures and options, bonds and gilts online. And there are brokers specialising in spread-betting and new investment vehicles, such as Exchange Traded Funds.

Meanwhile the educational and analytical resources available to the online investor continue to proliferate. And thanks to improvements in mobile communications we can transact and monitor our investments while on the move via internet-enabled mobile phones and hand-held organisers.

All this technology and information may not be able to guarantee that our investments will always go up, but it can make us better informed and better able to react when things aren't going so well.

What type of investor are you?

Not all brokers are the same. Some attempt to offer every service under the sun and provide a 'one-stop shop' for their customers, others offer a very simple service at low cost. Before shopping around for the right broker, think about the kind of investing you want to do. If you have no intention of buying options or investing in foreign equities, there is no advantage in choosing a broker that offers these services.

I've compiled a checklist of questions to help you decide what type of investor you are and what type of broker you are likely to need:

- Do you want access to a wide choice of investment products, such as funds, bonds and options, or are you happy just dealing in shares?

- Do you want as much research information as possible at your disposal on your broker's site, or are you happy to find it on other websites?

- Is it important to you to have access to live streaming share prices and news?

- Do you want the option to place orders in a variety of ways, including via telephone, interactive digital television or mobile device?

- Do you want access to foreign markets?

- Do you mind if your investments are held electronically in a nominee account on your behalf and you don't receive share certificates?

- How often are you likely to deal? Low dealing costs will be more important to frequent traders.

- Do you want to shelter your investments inside a tax-free Individual Savings Account?

- Are you sure you don't need one-to-one advice?

- What quality of telephone and/or e-mail support does the broker offer?

Charges

The good news for investors is that competition is so tough that brokers are having to mount loss-leading campaigns to woo new customers. For example, several brokers offer a month's commission-free trading. Some opportunistic investors happily open accounts, trade furiously within the free period, then simply stop or close the account and move on to the next broker offering free dealing. I wouldn't recommend this approach for novice investors, however.

As it is, average dealing charges have fallen over the last two years from around £20 to £30 per £1500 trade, to £10 to £15. But bear in mind that the dealing commission isn't the be-all and end-all of your decision. You may be an investor who is happy to buy just a few investments a year, so the dealing charge is less relevant to you. The average investor transacts less than ten times a year. So don't get hung up on the commission.

There are other less obvious charges to watch out for too, such as quarterly or annual administration fees, and fees for transferring stocks from one account to another. And if you fancy trading within a self-select ISA you should look closely at the broker's management charges. The same goes for Self-Invested Personal Pensions. Sometimes a broker may trumpet a low basic-dealing commission, only to recoup its money through higher charges elsewhere.

Of course, it's a different ball game for frequent traders. These are usually categorised as investors buying and selling shares more than thirty times a quarter, say. Brokers commonly reward these investors with lower dealing commissions. They often pay a fixed annual fee and a flat-rate dealing commission regardless of the size of the deal. Again, don't get carried away with this kind of offer. You may be making a false economy if you are tempted to deal more often than you should, making wrong investment decisions along the way. Protecting your capital is more important than saving on commission charges. Brokers want you to deal as often as you can because that's the way they make their money, but it isn't always the right thing to do.

For a start, on top of the dealing commission you pay stamp duty of 0.5 per cent on each purchase (not sales). Then you have to take into account the bid-offer spread – the difference between the price you can buy or sell a certain stock. An investor can be sitting on a 5 per cent loss immediately following a purchase once charges and the bid-offer spread have been taken into account. This means your shares have to do pretty well before you break even, let alone make a profit. The less time you give your shares to rise in value, the less likely it is that they will. So you have to be very skilled or very lucky to make money consistently from frequent trading. It is definitely not a practice for new investors with only a few thousand pounds to invest.

Traditionally, brokers adopted tiered commission structures, taking a percentage of the amount invested. This meant that the more you invested the more you paid in charges. Nowadays brokers have moved towards a flat-rate charging structure. Some just have one fixed fee, regardless of the size of the deal. This obviously favours wealthy investors. A £20,000 trade might have cost several hundred pounds in the bad old days, whereas some brokers would charge as little as £10 now. Other brokers still operate a tiered pricing structure, but maintain fixed charges within each band.

The move to flat-rate charging is welcome because it makes the whole dealing process more transparent and easy to understand for investors.

Interest rates

Investors often overlook the rate of interest paid on cash within an account. Most investors will keep a proportion of their capital in cash at any one time for security and to be ready if an investment opportunity presents itself. But how much interest are you getting on the money that is sitting idle? If you have a substantial cash fund, the difference between interest rates could be more important than the difference between dealing commissions. It is worth checking this out before committing yourself.

Taking a test drive

Many internet brokers now have demonstrations on their websites, enabling you to test out the services before you open an account. These are worth trying. It is important to get the feel of a service before you sign up. The site may be very sophisticated but poorly designed, or simply not your style. And how much online help do they provide? With competition so intense there might not be much to differentiate one broker from another apart from the usability and quality of its website.

Need help shopping around?

At the time of writing there were some thirty online brokers competing for the attentions of approximately 350,000 online investors. That's a lot of shopping around to do. Luckily, there are a few ratings and comparison services available to help you compare brokers on a like-for-like basis. Here are my two favourites:

BlueSky Ratings – www.blueskyratings.com

BlueSky is a European brokerage analyst that carries out exhaustive tests on hundreds of brokers. It examines a number of criteria, such as the range of services on offer and the usability of the websites. But BlueSky goes further. It also tests the brokers' telephone and e-mail response times. This is a very useful addition to the ratings because, as I've mentioned above, it is easy for investors to give too much prominence to the dealing charges and not enough to the quality of the customer service. Getting through on the phone when the website has crashed is probably more important than dealing charges for most investors.

FT YOUR MONEY 'BROKERFINDER' – http://ftyourmoney.ft.com/FTym/brokerfinder

FT Your Money's Brokerfinder is an admirably sophisticated search engine that lets you compare brokers according to a number of different criteria. It lists details of 135 brokerage accounts (brokers often have several different types of account). You say over what period you want to compare brokers, how many trades you might make per month and the likely size of the orders you'll place. Obviously these figures will vary, but it gives you a rough idea of the costs involved. You can choose whether you want an internet-only broker, or whether you want one that also has telephone dealing and/or a branch network. You can opt, too, for brokers that offer self-select Individual Savings Accounts.

Once you've made your selections, Brokerfinder provides a table listing the total costs over your chosen period. This takes administration charges into account as well. If you want to find out more about the full range of services a broker offers, simply click on the 'Details' link.

You should play around with the search criteria a few times to get a better idea of how competitive certain brokers really are. One broker may be suitable for a frequent trader, but not for an infrequent trader. One may have very cheap dealing facilities, but no self-select ISA facility. The *FT*'s Brokerfinder is a very useful tool to have at your disposal.

THE MOTLEY FOOL – www.fool.co.uk

The Motley Fool's 'Online Broker Centre' is not as comprehensive as Brokerfinder, featuring just eight online brokers. But the comparison table is useful nevertheless, as is Fool's round-up of the latest special offers. For example, in December 2001 e-Cortal was offering a generous £100 sign-up bonus to new account holders.

There's nothing to stop you having more than one online dealing account, especially if the administration charges are low, so this kind of special offer is worth knowing about.

MX MONEYEXTRA – www.moneyextra.com

Moneyextra provides a useful table of online brokers showing dealing commissions for three different deal sizes – £1000, £5000 and £25,000. There are details of administration charges, too, and other bells and whistles.

If you need advice

It is all very well learning how to choose your own investments and buy them online without any advice. But things get a lot trickier when the markets turn against you and your investments start to go down. Should you sell and buy back later when the shares are cheaper? Should you just buy more, taking advantage of the lower price? Or should you simply ignore such fluctuations completely and sit tight for the long term? These are tough questions and if everyone knew the answers we'd all be rich. A lot of investors still like to receive advice in these situations. So if you want to find a broker that also offers advice, go to the Association of Private Client Investment Managers & Stockbrokers (www.apcims.co.uk) website for a full list of its members.

How online dealing works

First you have to open an account. This can take minutes online with some and two weeks with others if they require paper-based proof of identity. After that you're usually issued with a user name and password or personal indentification number (PIN). This is to prevent anyone going online and buying shares in your name without your authority. Keeping your security details secret is your responsibility. If you lose or forget your password/PIN, most brokers will send it to you by e-mail so long as you can answer another pre-agreed security question.

You normally have to open the account with an initial deposit

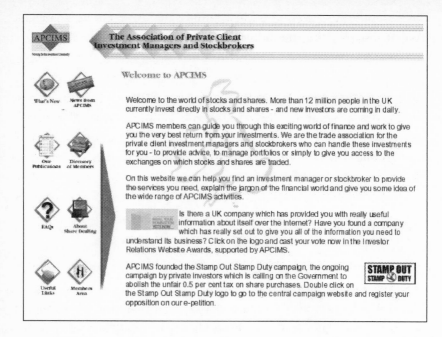

– some brokers impose a minimum. You can send this by cheque, set up a direct debit or standing order from your bank, or use a debit card to fund the account. If you set up a variable direct debit this gives you the freedom to transfer funds back and forth between your bank and share-dealing accounts very easily.

Once your account is up and running there's no necessity to invest straight away. As we suggested in the last chapter, setting up a 'fantasy portfolio' first can be a good way of learning the ropes and getting used to your broker's research tools. Once you are happy to trade, the process is quite simple. You usually enter the stock market code of the company you want to buy or sell (there's usually a 'look-up' facility if you don't know it) and enter the number of shares or the amount you want to invest.

The best brokers will then give you a live price quote that you can either accept or reject. If you like the price, press 'enter'. Most brokers also give you the opportunity to place a 'limit order' where you can specify the price you want to deal at. Normally this is on a 'fill or kill' basis, which means that the deal is cancelled if it can't be completed at the price you want. Some brokers will keep limit orders open until the end of the trading day. This facility also means you can place orders out of market hours, at the weekend, say.

When you've entered your order you're normally given a last chance to review it and make sure you haven't made a mistake. Check over the details carefully – there's no going back after this point. If you're happy, press the 'submit' button. Your order is then processed instantaneously (unless there is some reason why it has to be completed manually by the broker – if it is outside 'Normal Market Size', for example). You then receive a unique order number to prove that the transaction was made and executed, and are sent an electronic contract note recording the terms on which the deal was made. It's a good idea to print these off.

Is it safe?

All trades are scrambled using 128-bit encryption – the strongest security currently allowed – before they are sent. This means that it is virtually impossible for anyone to intercept and decipher confidential information as it is sent across the web. Brokers also have sophisticated 'firewall' security protecting their computer systems from unauthorised infiltration. It is extremely unlikely that anyone would be able to gain access to your account, unless you were careless about protecting your security details.

One major advantage of online trading is that it is easy to keep audit trails of all actions taken by investor and broker. Having said that, it is a good idea to print off confirmations of trades even if they are stored on the broker's own systems. If something does go badly wrong, most reputable brokers are covered by some sort of insurance that protects client funds from theft or fraud.

Round-up of the best brokers

Brokers are changing their fee structures, merging and being taking over so quickly these days that this section of the book is likely to be out of date fairly quickly. This is why I've suggested some online resources to help you. As we all know, the web is far better at keeping databases up to date than the printed word.

What follows are reviews of a cross-section of the best brokers chosen according to functionality, value for money and suitability for different types of investor. The brokers are listed in alphabetical order.

AMERICAN EXPRESS SHAREPEOPLE –
www.sharepeople.com

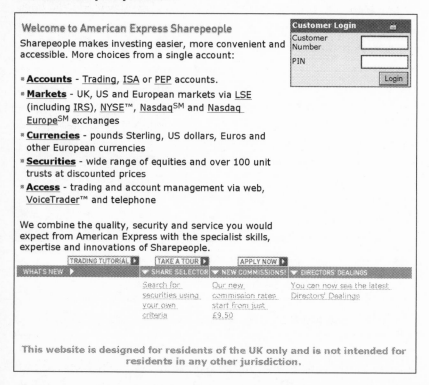

Welcome to American Express Sharepeople

Sharepeople makes investing easier, more convenient and accessible. More choices from a single account:

* **Accounts** - Trading, ISA or PEP accounts.
* **Markets** - UK, US and European markets via LSE (including IRS), NYSE™, Nasdaq^{SM} and Nasdaq Europe^{SM} exchanges
* **Currencies** - pounds Sterling, US dollars, Euros and other European currencies
* **Securities** - wide range of equities and over 100 unit trusts at discounted prices
* **Access** - trading and account management via web, VoiceTrader™ and telephone

We combine the quality, security and service you would expect from American Express with the specialist skills, expertise and innovations of Sharepeople.

Customer Login
Customer Number
PIN
Login

TRADING TUTORIAL ▶   TAKE A TOUR ▶   APPLY NOW ▶

WHAT'S NEW ▶   ▼ SHARE SELECTOR   ▼ NEW COMMISSIONS!   ▼ DIRECTORS' DEALINGS

Search for securities using your own criteria

Our new commission rates start from just £9.50

You can now see the latest Directors' Dealings

This website is designed for residents of the UK only and is not intended for residents in any other jurisdiction.

Sharepeople is a stand-alone internet-only broker originally backed by a consortium including Goldman Sachs and GE Capital. It has now been taken over by American Express, which at least might secure its immediate financial future. It offers a number of sophisticated features, including international dealing in a range of currencies (dollars, Euros and sterling), ISA and PEP accounts, and access to over 100 unit trusts and open-ended investment companies. You deal online and by telephone. Research facilities include a 'share selector' tool to help you find shares that suit your investment objectives and details of directors' share dealings. Dealing commissions are reasonable, making for a good all-round package.

BARCLAYS STOCKBROKERS – **www.barclays-stockbrokers.co.uk**

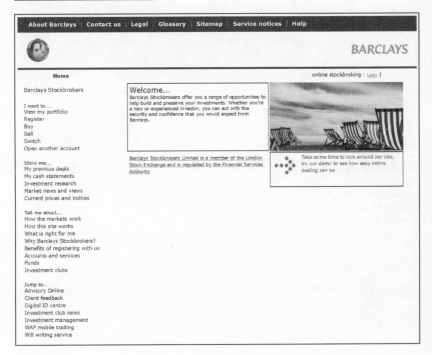

Barclays Stockbrokers will suit the type of investor who likes to have most services in one easily accessible place and the security of knowing there's a big bank and a large branch network supporting the online dealing operation. Barclays will seldom feature in the 'lowest dealing commission' lists, however, so it is less suitable for frequent traders.

But Barclays was one of the first brokers to offer online access to investment funds and it incorporates other innovations into its service. For example, you can sell one share and buy another in one transaction and for one dealing commission. Barclays also uses its size – it is the largest retail stockbroker in the UK – to negotiate better prices for your shares from the market makers. It offers access to advisory services and self-select ISAs too. Some investors also like having access to their bank accounts under the same roof. Where Barclays falls down is in its lack of sophisticated investment research resources.

CHARLES SCHWAB EUROPE – www.schwab-europe.com

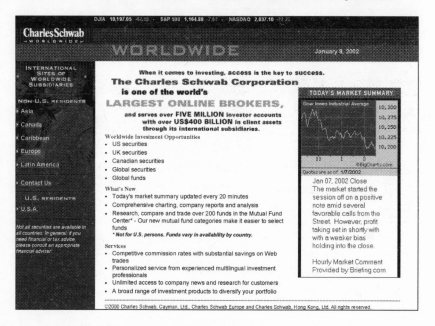

Charles Schwab Europe is one of the UK's largest online brokers. It offers dealing by computer and telephone (including automated touch-tone trading) and has a well-deserved reputation for being first with innovative services. For example, it was the first broker to allow investors to manage self-select Individual Savings Accounts online, to trade in options, and among the first to offer trading in US stocks. Most of its news and research data is supplied by Reuters. There are several accounts, the most basic being MarketMaster. Serious investors can join the Frequent Traders Club and enjoy flat-rate trading for an annual fee. If you want to invest in US stocks you have to set up a dollar-denominated account.

As in the US, Schwab is never the cheapest service around, but at least you know you're dealing with a company that has a great deal of experience in offering electronic trading. It is also spending a lot of money recruiting call centre support staff, since it realises that even independent online investors need help sometimes. Schwab's commitment to a multi-channel customer service approach makes it ideal for the novice investor who wants to get serious. The educational resources are excellent – you get what you pay for.

COMDIRECT – www.comdirect.co.uk

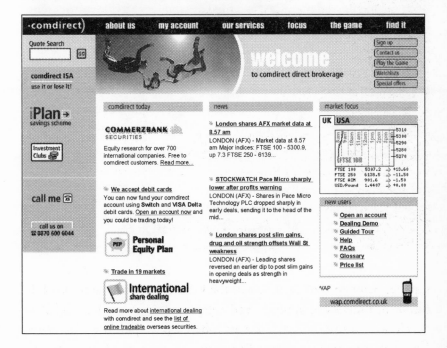

Owned by German banking giant Commerzbank, Comdirect is a relative newcomer to the UK. Its site is refreshingly simple in design, and its fee structure pleasingly straightforward and one of the most competitive around. But don't be deceived. Comdirect's service is impressively sophisticated. It offers trading in nineteen international markets and research on over 700 companies. You have access to investment funds online, plus innovative savings schemes involving exchange-traded funds. These are index-tracking funds that can be bought and sold online just like shares and kept within a self-select ISA. There is also support for investment clubs and ISAs and PEPS. The only concern is over its commercial viability. Its parent was thinking of closing the UK operation due to lack of demand, but changed its mind. Let's just hope Comdirect weathers the current downturn and sticks around.

DEAL4FREE.COM – www.deal4free.com

Deal4free.com, the brainchild of CMC, a well-respected futures, options and currency trader, is aimed at sophisticated investors who understand the stock market and the nature of risk. It offers commission-free dealing with no stamp duty either by using financial instruments called 'contracts for difference' (CFDs). You don't actually buy the underlying shares, just the price of them, so there are no dealing charges. You also buy on a 20 per cent margin. This means that if you want to buy £1000's worth of shares you deposit £200 with CMC. This can magnify your gains, but also your losses, so it's not for the faint-hearted. Profits are transferred to the customer's account within twenty-four hours. If you keep the CFD shares overnight you pay financing costs to CMC, as if you'd borrowed the whole amount (not just the margin cost). You have to have at least £5000 to open an account and CMC can only provide execution-only services to investors classed as 'non-private'. This means customers have to show CMC's compliance department they have trading experience.

DLJ DIRECT – www.dljdirect.co.uk

At the time of writing DLJ Direct was in the process of being taken over by T.D. Waterhouse, the Canadian online brokerage with a UK operation. The site may have changed by the time this book is published. That warning aside, DLJ aims to service high-net-worth individuals with fast, efficient dealing backed up by solid research. It has always been innovative, introducing online account opening and account funding via debit card, for example. There is a wide range of investment products on offer, including international

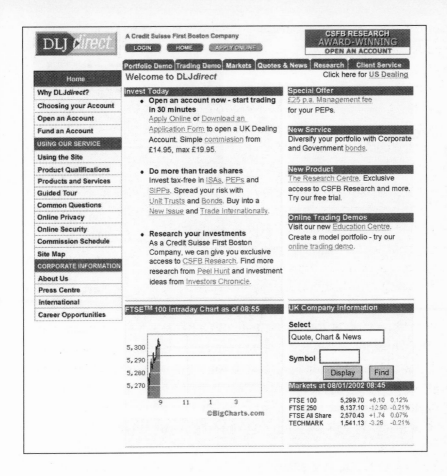

shares, ISAs, self-invested personal pensions and bonds (telephone trading only). DLJ is not the cheapest broker but it is not the most expensive either. Check out the US version of the site (www.dljdirect.com) and compare the types of services on offer. You'll see how sophisticated the UK service could become in time.

E-CORTAL – www.e-cortal.com

e-Cortal, owned by French bank BNP Paribas, was the first of the European brokers to set up a service for UK customers. It offers an impressive international dealing service covering nine stock markets around the world. At this stage, though, the range of stocks you can invest in on each market is not comprehensive. For example, on the

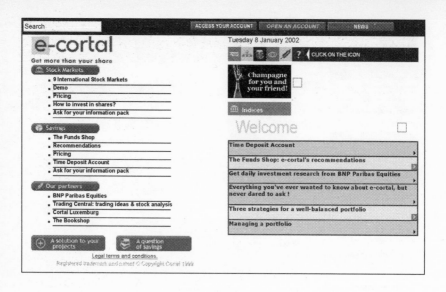

London markets you can only invest in FTSE 350 stocks rather than the whole lot. But this is likely to improve as e-Cortal becomes more established. The range of research resources is also fairly limited, but the service is very cheap, given its transnational sophistication. You get access to European funds too. Accounts are denominated in Euros and there's no minimum opening balance required.

E*TRADE UK – www.etrade.co.uk

E*Trade, another of the US brokers, has made a name for itself as a purely electronic service (back-up telephone dealing is supplied when the internet system breaks down). Frequent traders get access to live streaming prices and news plus dealing commissions from £8.95, making it a suitable candidate for serious investors. New investors can set up fantasy portfolios and gain access to the research for around £5 a month before setting up an account proper. You can deal in US stocks if you set up a dollar-denominated account and make use of the London Stock Exchange's new service involving Crest Depository Interest forms. With CDIs you can Trade in 112 European and five US securities from eleven international markets.

Research facilities are excellent. E*Trade has teamed up with

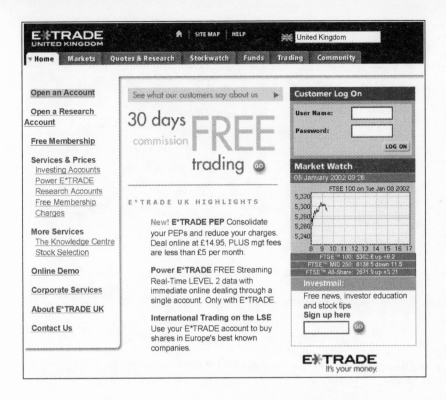

Digitallook.com to provide stock selection tools. Investors can search for stocks using a number of financial criteria, such as dividends, price/earnings/growth (PEG) and market capitalisation. Shares are given risk grades too and you can easily look at recent news stories about companies you're interested in. E*Trade also has a lively bulletin board populated by fellow investors who are never short of investment opinions and ideas.

FasTrade – https://www.fastrade.co.uk

This is the no-frills execution-only online service from traditional regional broker Torrie & Co. Dealing commissions are reasonably low, and it offers access to international markets and the UK's smaller markets, Ofex and the Alternative Investment Market. You can invest in funds too. This is one for investors happy to receive most of their research facilities from other websites.

0.5% commission   FASTRADE

Please take a moment to read our disclaimer by clicking on the link at the bottom of this page. You must do this to gain access to the FasTrade website.

Welcome To FasTrade

- FasTrade is the execution-only internet dealing service of Torrie & Co stockbrokers.
- We are independent stockbrokers established in 1910 and the last independent partnership remaining in Scotland.
- Torrie & Co's main site gives you more information on the firm and our other services.

We Offer

- Real time dealing on Internet, ISAs, General and Single Company PEP accounts.
- Immediate confirmation of transactions.
- Low commission dealing.
- A strong commitment to customer service.
- The ability to place orders 24 hours a day through our site.

- Improved prices on many of your trades.
- The ability to send us orders manually.
- Dealing on the AIM, OFEX and foreign markets.
- Dealing in unit trusts.
- Limit minding.
- No joining fee.

If you have not read our disclaimer then please do so by clicking on the link below. You must do this to enter the FasTrade website.

(index)

disclaimer

Fastrade is the internet dealing service of Torrie & Co.
Torrie & Co is an Independent Private Client Stockbroker
Member of the London Stock Exchange

FIMATEX – www.fimatex.co.uk

At fimatex.co.uk we've brought together all the elements and support you need to trade online.

GTS

click logo to start GTS demo

Welcome to the Fimatex web-site!

- Test drive our service free for five days.
  Click on this link for more details.

- Buy and sell UK shares at extremely competitive commission rates.

- US trading from your sterling account with the option to upgrade to Real Time Prices.
  Click on this link for more details.

- Keep yourself informed with our new alerting service.
  Click on this link for more details.

- GTS, our powerful Windows® based trading tool is now available in the UK.
  Click on this link for more details.

Fimatex is another European broker owned by French bank Société Générale. It has been trying to break into the UK market at a particularly tough time – especially difficult when your brand is completely unknown. Fimatex emphasises the speed and reliability of its dealing technology. The system allows dealing in US stocks from a sterling-denominated account rather than the usual dollar account. You can deal online or via telephone (although telephone dealing is more expensive). Commission rates are competitive and you can upgrade your service to receive real-time UK and US share prices should you want them. Fimatex also produces its own trading software costing £150 (free for new investors under a special offer at the time of writing). Serious investors load it on to their PCs to give them a Windows trading environment in which to view charts and fundamental financial data online. My only concern about this broker is about the level of financial commitment from its parent. Will it still be around in a year's time?

HALIFAX SHAREDEALING – www.sharexpress.co.uk

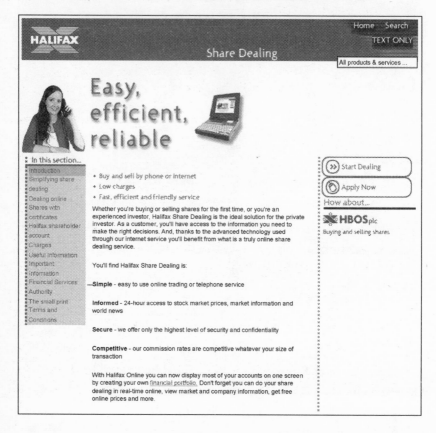

It was only a matter of time before Halifax added an online share-dealing service to its existing telephone-dealing service. Called ShareXpress, it is very much aimed at the mass market – relatively unsophisticated investors looking for a very simple, accessible dealing service. Research tools are limited to company and markets news, plus the usual share prices. If you're happy to get your in-depth research elsewhere, ShareXpress is a competitively priced service – the minimum commission is one of the lowest and there are no management or administration charges whatsoever. But there's no facility to deal in foreign stocks or within a self-select ISA.

HARGREAVES LANSDOWN –
www.hargreaveslansdown.co.uk

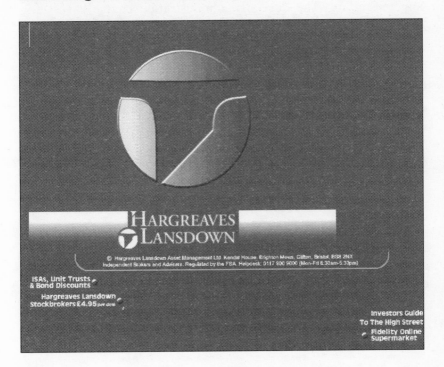

Hargreaves Lansdown's brokerage service is extremely competitively priced with a flat rate of £9.95 per trade. It has recently introduced limited international online dealing in 150 stocks (over 5000 US and European stocks are available to telephone investors) from sterling-denominated accounts. The broker provides market information, access to its own analyst reports, three share-tipping newsletters from its research team, plus a monthly newsletter containing its latest news and views.

IDEALING – <u>www.idealing.co.uk</u>

Lord knows how this broker makes any money, but as long as it lasts it represents terrific value for frequent traders and investors dealing in large amounts. iDealing charges just £10 for any size of trade whether you're buying UK, US or EU stocks. You can trade internationally from one sterling account, too, and dividends are paid in sterling. The quarterly administration charge is just £5. iDealing also offers a self-select ISA and PEP transfer facility. The only downside is that the broker provides no research facilities of its own, just links to other websites. As high-quality research is only a few mouse clicks away, this may seem a small price to pay for such a cost-effective service. A low-cost, no-frills operation has worked for the discount airline companies; it will be interesting to see if it can work for online brokerages.

IMIWEB – www.imiweb.co.uk

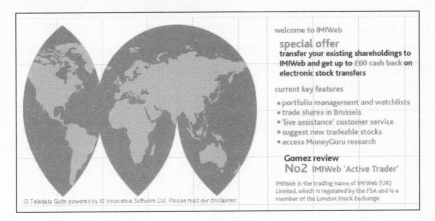

IMIWeb is another astonishingly low-cost newcomer offering international trading in seven markets from one sterling account. UK dealing costs just £10, international dealing costs £15 (plus a small charge to cover foreign exchange costs), and there are no administration charges whatsoever. It is the best deal around, particularly for wealthy investors who like to invest big chunks at a time. Research resources are limited to company and markets news stories through partnerships with AFX, Standard & Poors and Reuters, among others. If it can survive commercially with such a competitive offering, IMIWeb should be a big hit.

JAMES BREARLEY & SONS – www.jbrearley.co.uk

The traditional regional brokers are also getting in on the act these days. Brearley's execution-only service is called Icon, but investors who prefer a little hand-holding in the management of their investments will appreciate the advisory and discretionary services to hand as well. It's not the cheapest or the best, but could suit more old-fashioned investors.

KILLIK & CO. – www.killik.co.uk

Welcome to Killik & Co

Interested? Email us now on ...
events@killik.co.uk

Killik & Co is an independent firm offering Stockbroking services in addition to high quality investment and financial planning advice. Through a branch network we aim to build a long-standing relationship with our clients based on integrity, trust and accessibility. Killik & Co welcomes all types of investor and has no minimum portfolio requirement.

Welcome to our website. If you are a regular visitor to our site you will notice a number of changes, especially with regard to where you may now find certain pages that you frequently visit. Please find below instructions on the new location of three key areas. You may like to set up new bookmarks for your favourite pages.

Your **Account Online** - this can be accessed through the Client Area button at the top of the screen - which will also give you access to our online Research. You can log in to this area from any point on the site. However, for a link straight through to the Account Online login page **click here**.

Research Online - this also should be accessed through the Client Area where a password is required. Clients can apply online for access.

Daily View - the latest edition of the Daily View can be reached by clicking on the banner at the bottom of this page or selecting Daily View under the Research heading.

Similarly, Killik & Co. is a traditional UK stockbroker that has incorporated online dealing into its range of services without giving up its advisory role. This means investors pay above average dealing commission – a minimum £30 per deal – but you can talk to one of its broking team about your investment ideas whenever you like. Killik wants to avoid the execution-only route and maintain a personal relationship with each client. Whether this strategy will survive in an environment where more and more cheap execution-only brokers are entering the market remains to be seen. The online dealing facility is just viewed as an added-value service for customers. Killik specialises in researching smaller companies and less mainstream investment opportunities and, in this regard, its briefing notes are very good. So if you think you would like advice on building up a portfolio but you still want the option to deal on your own, Killik offers the best of both worlds – at a price.

MY**BROKER** – www.mybroker.com

*my***BROKER**
Enigma

Welcome

myBroker Enigma. **Click** on the image above for myBroker's new dynamic trading signals.

Existing myBroker Enigma subscribers **Click here**.

"myBroker is technically one of the most advanced of the online brokers!" - Financial Times

myBroker is the ultimate DIRECT ACCESS system for the online investor. One of the many unique advantages myBroker has over its competitors is on just one screen and with one account, you have the ability to create and protect your portfolio utilising LIVE streaming market data, comprehensive technical analysis (AIQ Charting) and fundamental company data - for UK, US and European stock markets.

There are just 2 steps to join the tens of thousands who are trading UK, US and European stock markets with the greatest LIVE online shares, options and futures trading service at their fingertips.

1 - Install myBroker free-of-charge
2 - Open a trading account

Click here for myBroker's new dynamic trading signals.

This is a very sophisticated trading service from a company called Options Direct, a specialist in equities and derivatives. Investors download special software on to their PCs capable of handling a multitude of live information 'feeds' from international stock markets. You can order a CD-ROM instead if you prefer. The 'live' environment may be a little intimidating for novice investors but is perfect for experienced day traders. There is a bewildering choice of news and data services to help you with your research, yet dealing commission starts from just £12.50 and there are no set-up or administration fees. You can personalise the trading screen to monitor your favourite shares and trade in futures and options too. myBroker is a serious proposition for the full-time investor.

Nothing Ventured – www.nothing-ventured.com

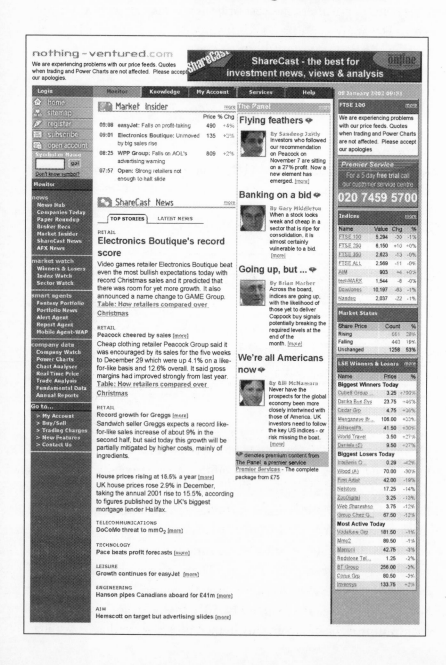

This superbly resourced brokerage was set up by Durlacher, a quoted UK research consultancy and investment company specialising in new media and technology. It is a very switched-on site designed to suit high-net-worth investors looking for new investment opportunities, especially in the emerging technology sector. The analysis and research facilities are top-rate. Investment tools include news round-ups, e-mail alerts when a share price meets your target buying or selling price and sophisticated share price performance charts. There is a wealth of investment research and comment, international dealing facilities, plus the chance to manage your own self-invested personal pension online. The site was awarded top slot for October 2001 by BlueSky Ratings, the European Brokerage analyst. For such a well-stocked site, the dealing commissions are pretty reasonable.

STOCKTRADE – www.stocktrade.co.uk

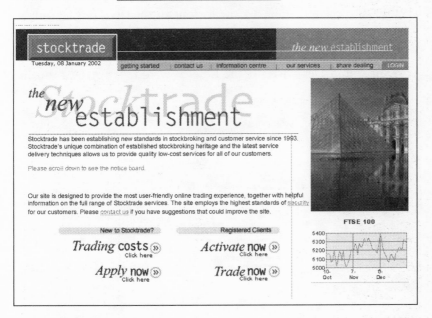

Stocktrade is the internet and telephone-dealing division of Brewin Dolphin Securities, a well-known traditional stockbroker. Stocktrade was the first company in the UK to offer real-time dealing online, but has suffered a little by not having the vast marketing budgets of its US rivals. It was slow adding research facilities to its service, but it has since done so, including daily market analysis from its parent and all the latest company news and results. There are price and performance data, plus graphing facilities. Stocktrade has also recently added contracts for difference trading to its range of services (see Deal4Free's review above for an explanation of CFDs). Stocktrade's service is impressive for its live share price environment – most brokers show prices delayed by fifteen minutes and charge extra for live prices. Stocktrade customers have to apply for personal membership of Crest, the electronic share settlement system, which means their names stay on the stock register, unlike in a nominee account. Deals are settled the day after each trade (T+1).

T. D. WATERHOUSE – www.tdwaterhouse.co.uk

This is a surprisingly unflashy site for one of the UK's largest online brokers. The Canadian company aggressively entered the UK market by snaffling up other brokerages, such as Sharemarket, YorkShare and Dealwise. At the time of writing it was also in the

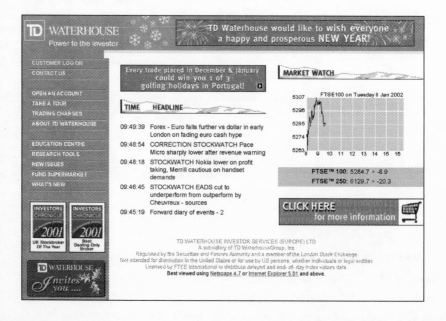

process of taking over DLJdirect. Voted 'Best Dealing Only Broker' and 'Overall Stockbroker of the Year' 2001 by *Investors Chronicle* readers, it must be doing something right. It is simply designed yet has most of the features you would want from a one-stop-shop broker, including education and research tools plus access to a 'fund supermarket' as well as equities. It also offers certificated trading for those who are unwilling to accept the electronic world entirely just yet, although this is more expensive and settlement takes ten days. T.D. Waterhouse operates a tiered flat-rate commission structure and lower commissions for frequent traders. International dealing is by telephone only.

Warning

Buying and selling shares online is very fast and easy to do. This has the advantage of enabling investors to react quickly to news and events, but it can also encourage investors to behave rashly and deal impetuously. This is a sure-fire way of losing money fast. Make certain your investment decisions are thoroughly researched and that you don't deal more often than you should. Investing online can become addictive, so unless you can afford to lose a lot of money, treat the technology with caution.

5

Investing
Internationally

Introduction

As we've seen in the last chapter, a growing number of online brokers are incorporating international dealing into their services, several with sterling-denominated accounts too. Two years ago you would have had to open an account with a US or European brokerage direct, fill in heaps of forms and pay handsomely for the privilege. We've come on a long way since then. The introduction of the Euro has helped to harmonise European trading and make it more accessible to UK investors, while improved co-operation between international stock exchanges and settlement systems has opened up a whole new world of opportunity.

But why invest internationally? Put simply, there are some fantastic foreign companies out there performing much better than many UK stocks. They could be helping your portfolio to grow even faster. What's more, you get a far greater choice of stocks to invest in, giving you wider scope to try out investment ideas.

Investment experts also believe in the concept of spreading risk. That doesn't just mean investing in different companies, it means investing across different economies too. If you only invest in UK companies and the UK suffers a recession, the likelihood is that your portfolio will suffer. Economies are rarely synchronised, so if the UK is in recession, the US may be enjoying a boom time and vice versa. If you spread your portfolio of investments across different economies, you reduce the risk of *all* your stocks performing badly at the same time.

Another reason is that dealing commissions can be lower, especially in the US, where brokers enjoy such large volumes of trades that they can afford to operate on wafer-thin profit margins. Some brokers offer online dealing from $5. Also, you don't pay 0.5 per cent stamp duty on share purchases as you do in the UK. And US brokers tend to be more reliable, with fewer service interruptions.

Before you start to buy foreign stocks, however, bear in mind that there are over thirty US companies already listed on the London Stock Exchange, so you don't necessarily have to buy abroad to get access to foreign companies.

American Depository Receipts (ADRs)

The main instrument for investing abroad has traditionally been the American Depository Receipt (ADR). These are dollar-denominated securities backed by the underlying company stock. The price of the ADR and the company's share usually shadow each other. They are a convenient way for foreign investors to buy into the stock market of the world's most successful economy without the fuss of setting up separate brokerage accounts in different currencies and using different languages. Lots of other foreign companies list ADRs on the US exchanges, so you can get access to global stocks this way, not just US and British stocks.

They are traded like any other US security and so you pay no stamp duty on purchases (as you do in the UK) and can also benefit from US brokerage rates, which are often far lower than ours ($5 per deal in some cases). UK companies often issue ADRs and it can be cheaper buying these than their UK-listed shares. It sounds crazy but it's true.

The main drawback is the currency risk associated with

converting from dollars to sterling. But if you assign a proportion of your capital to ADRs and are happy to keep the money in dollars for a significant period, you should be able to minimise the conversion costs. There is also the chance that the exchange rate may move in your favour, exaggerating your profits.

As mentioned above, you used to have to open an account with a US broker to buy ADRs. You don't have to now, as the number of UK brokers offering international dealing is growing fast. If you plan to trade heavily in the US, however, it may still be worth opening a dedicated US account to benefit from their lower dealing charges.

You can find a list of all the available ADRs on a site called Global Investor (www.global-investor.com). They are grouped by the underlying company's country of origin. Other sites worth looking at for research into ADRs include Worldly Investor (www.worldlyinvestor.com) and ADR (www.adr.com), run by J. P. Morgan, the investment bank.

International Retail Service (IRS)

Thanks to greater co-operation between Crest, the company that operates the electronic settlement system for shares in the UK, and its foreign counterparts, a new service has been launched that gives UK investors access to foreign stocks simply and cheaply. Called the International Retail Service, the system is based on Crest Depository Interest forms. These are similar to ADRs in that investors get the benefit of the underlying companies without the hassle of owning the equities direct.

So far the IRS includes 117 stocks listed in the following countries:

Belgium	Netherlands
Canada	Spain
Finland	Sweden
France	Switzerland
Germany	United States
Italy	

The list of available stocks is shown here:

ABN Amro	AAB	Netherlands
Accor SA EUR3	ACO	France
ACG	ACG	Germany
Activcard	AVD	France
Adecco SA	ADO	Switzerland
Adidas-Salomon	ADI	Germany
Aegon	AGN	Netherlands
AEM SPA	AEM	Italy
Ahlers prefs	AAH	Germany
Ahold	AHD	Netherlands
Air Liquid	AIL	France
AKZO	AKZ	Netherlands
Alcatel	ATT	France
Alcoa Inc	ALI	United States
Alleanza Assicrazioni Spa	ALL	Italy
Allianz	ALZ	Germany
Alstom EUR6	ALS	France
Amazon Com Inc	AZZ	United States
American Express Co	AMX	United States
AOL Time Warner Inc	AOL	United States
Articon Integralis	AIT	Germany
ASM Lithography	AMM	Netherlands
Assurances Gen. De France(AGF) NPV	AFF	France
AT&T Corp	ATC	United States
Autostrade Spa	AOE	Italy
Aventis	AVN	France
Axa	AXA	France
Baloise Hldgs	BAL	Switzerland
Banca Di Roma	BDR	Italy
Banca Fideuram	BCF	Italy
Banca Monte Dei Paschi De Sienna	BPS	Italy
Banca Nazionale Del Lavoro	BL.	Italy
Banco Bilboa Vizcaya Argentaria EUR0.49	BVA	Spain
Banco Santander Central Hispano EUR0.50	BDS	Spain
BASF	BFA	Germany
Bayer	BYR	Germany
Bayerische HypoVereinsbank	BAH	Germany
Bertrandt	BRR	Germany
Beru	BZL	Germany
BHW Holding	BWW	Germany
Bipop-Carire	BPC	Italy

BMP	BMP	Germany
BMW	BMW	Germany
BNP Paribas	BNP	France
Boeing Co	BOE	United States
Bouygues	BUG	France
Brokat	BSA	Germany
Buhrmann NV EUR1.2(POST CONS)	BUH	Netherlands
Bulgari Spa	BUL	Italy
Canal +	CNL	France
CAP Gemini	CAG	France
Cargolifter	COF	Germany
Carrefour	CFR	France
Casino Guichard-Perrachon EUR1.53	CGD	France
Caterpillar Inc	CTA	United States
Cenit Systemhaus	CIT	Germany
Ciba Speciality Chemicals Inc	CBN	Switzerland
Cisco Systems	CSC	United States
Citigroup Inc	CGP	United States
Clariant	CRN	Switzerland
Coca Cola Co	CCA	United States
Comdirect Bank AG	CDR	Germany
Commerzbank	CZB	Germany
Compagne De Saint-Gobain EUR16	COD	France
Compaq Computer Corp	COP	United States
Consors Disc.-Broker AG	CNB	Germany
Credit Lyonnais	CYO	France
Credit Suisse Group CHF20(REGD)	CRD	Switzerland
DAB Bank AG	DBA	Germany
Daimler Chrysler	DCX	Germany
Dassault Systemes EUR1	DAS	France
Degussa NPV	DEG	Germany
Dell Computers	DEC	United States
Deutsche Bank	DBK	Germany
Dexia	DEX	France
DIS	DDE	Germany
Dresdner Bank	DRB	Germany
DSM	DSM	Netherlands
Dupont (EI) De Nemours & Co	DUP	United States
E.ON	EON	Germany
Eastman Kodak Co	EKD	United States
Easy Software	ESW	Germany
Elan Corp	ELAD	United States

Elmos Semiconductor	ELG	Germany
Elsevier	ELS	Netherlands
EM.TV Merchandising AG	ETV	Germany
EMC Corp Massachusetts	EMC	United States
EMS-Chemie Hldg AG	ECE	Switzerland
Endesa SA EUR1.2(REGD)	END	Spain
Enel	ENE	Italy
ENI	ENA	Italy
Epcos AG Ord NPV	ESS	Germany
Ericsson	ERI	Sweden
European Aeronautic Defense and Space3	EAD	Netherlands
Evotec	EVO	Germany
Exxon Mobil Corp	EXX	United States
Fiat Spa	FIA	Italy
Fielmann	FIE	Germany
Finmeccanica Spa	FNA	Italy
Fortis	FOT	Netherlands
France Telecom	FTE	France
Fresenius Medica Care NPV	FUA	Germany
General Electric Co	GEC	United States
General Motors Corp	GMR	United States
Generali	GER	Italy
Getronics NV EUR0.04	GTT	Netherlands
Givaudan AG	GIV	Switzerland
Groupe Danone	DNN	France
Gruppo Edit L'espresso	GEL	Italy
Gucci Group NV NLG2.23 ORD	GUC	Netherlands
Hagemeyer EUR1.2	HAG	Netherlands
Hawesko	HAW	Germany
Heineken	HEI	Netherlands
Henkel Kgaa Non-V Prf NPV	HEK	Germany
Hewlett Packard Co	HEW	United States
Heyde	HEY	Germany
Holcim	HIM	Switzerland
Holding Parteipazioni Industriazi	HDP	Italy
Home Depot Inc	HOM	United States
Honeywell Intl. Inc	HON	United States
InfineonTechnologies AG Ord NPV	IFO	Germany
ING	ING	Netherlands
Intel	ICO	United States
International Bus Mach Corp	IBM	United States
International Paper Co	IPP	United States

Intershop Comm	INC	Germany
Intesabci Spa EUR0.52	IAB	Italy
Iona Technologies	IOND	United States
Italgas	IAS	Italy
Ixos	IXS	Germany
Johnson & Johnson	JJJ	United States
JP Morgan Chase & Co	JPM	United States
Julius Baer Hldgs AG	JUB	Switzerland
KPN	KPN	Netherlands
KPNQWEST	KWT	Netherlands
Kudelski SA	KUD	Switzerland
L' Oreal	LOL	France
Lafarge	LFG	France
Lagardere S.C.A. FF40(REGD)	LAG	France
Linde AG NPV	LDE	Germany
Linos	LIN	Germany
Lintec Computer	LIC	Germany
Lonza Group AGN	LNA	Switzerland
Lucent Technologies	LUT	United States
Lufthansa	LHA	Germany
LVMH	LVM	France
Man AG Ord NPV	MAG	Germany
McDonalds Corp	MCD	United States
Mediaset	MEP	Italy
Mediobanca Spa	MEO	Italy
Mediolanum	ME.	Italy
Merck & Co Inc	MRK	United States
Metro AG Ord NPV	MEE	Germany
Michelin	MIH	France
Microsoft	MSF	United States
Minnesota Mining & Man.(MMM)	MMM	United States
Mobilicom AG	MOM	Germany
Motorola Inc	MOT	United States
Munich Reinsurance	MUN	Germany
Nasdaq 100 Trust	QQQ	United States
Nemetschek	NEK	Germany
Neschen	NSN	Germany
Nestle	NSTR	Switzerland
Nokia	NOK	Finland
Nordea AB EUR0.39632(SEK)	NOE	Sweden
Nortel Networks Corp	NNC	United States
Novartis	NOV	Switzerland

NTL Inc	NTL	United States
Numico	NUC	Netherlands
Olivetti Spa EUR1	OLI	Italy
Oracle	ORL	United States
Palm Inc	PAL	United States
Peugeot	PEU	France
Pfeiffer Vacuum	PVT	Germany
Pfizer Inc	PFZ	United States
Philip Morris Cos Inc	MOP	United States
Philips	PLE	Netherlands
Pinault Printemps	PPP	France
Pirelli Spa	PLA	Italy
Popnet Internet	PNZ	Germany
Preussag AG NPV	PRK	Germany
Proctor & Gamble Co	PGM	United States
Puma	PUM	Germany
RAS	RAZ	Italy
Rational	RAA	Germany
Renault	RNT	France
Repsol-YPF SA EUR1	REP	Spain
Richemont AG	RIT	Switzerland
Roche	ROG	Switzerland
Rolo Banca 1473 Spa	ROB	Italy
Royal Dutch	RYD	Netherlands
RWE	RWW	Germany
Sair Group	SAO	Switzerland
Sampo-Leonia OYJ	SA.	Finland
San Paolo	SPP	Italy
Sanofi	SNF	France
SAP AG ST O.N.	SAP	Germany
SBC Communications Inc	SBC	United States
Schering AG NPV	SCG	Germany
Schneider Electr. EUR8	SCH	France
Seat-Pagine Gialle	SEE	Italy
Serono SA	SBI	Switzerland
Siemens	SIE	Germany
Singulus Technol AG	SIL	Germany
Sixt ord	SKT	Germany
Societe Gen.De Surveill.Hldg.SA	SG.	Switzerland
Societe Generale	SGN	France
Sodexho Alliance EUR4	SXH	France
Sonera	SRA	Finland

ST MicroElectronics	SME	France
Suez Lvonnais	SUE	France
Sulzer AG	SUL	Switzerland
Sun Microsystems	SUW	United States
Swatch Group	SWH	Switzerland
Swatch Group	SWR	Switzerland
Swiss Life	SWF	Switzerland
Swiss Reinsurance CHF10(REGD)	SWI	Switzerland
Swisscom AG CHF25(REGD)	SMO	Switzerland
T-Online Intern AG	TEI	Germany
T.I.M. SPA	TIM	Italy
Telecom Italia	TCL	Italy
Telefonica SA EUR1	TDE	Spain
Television Francaise (T.F.1) EUR0.20	TFR	France
Terra (Lycos) Networks	TRR	Spain
Thomson Multimedia EUR3.75	TMM	France
Thyssenkrupp AG NPV	THK	Germany
TNT Post	TNT	Netherlands
Total Fina Elf	TOF	France
UBS AG CHF2.80(REGD)	UBS	Switzerland
Unaxis Hldg AG	UXS	Switzerland
Unicredito	UNC	Italy
Unilever NV CVA NFI I	UNL	Netherlands
United Technologies Corp	UTC	United States
UPC	UPC	Netherlands
Utimaco Safeware	UTI	Germany
Valeo EUR3	VAE	France
Versatel Telecom Intl.NV Ord NLG 0.05	VTE	Netherlands
Vivendi	VIV	France
VNU	VNU	Netherlands
Volkswagen	VKW	Germany
Walmart Stores Inc	WAL	United States
Wanadoo	WAN	France
Wolters Kluwer	WKL	Netherlands
XO Communications	XOC	United States
Yahoo Inc	YAH	United States

The number of stocks included in the IRS should grow as the electronic links between exchanges and settlement systems improves over time.

ADVANTAGES OF INVESTING IN IRS STOCKS

The good news about IRS-listed stocks is that most of them can also be held within an ISA, PEP or Self-invested Personal Pension (SIPP), and bought and sold through online brokers at the same price as conventional shares. Some brokers will only allow the US stocks to be bought over the phone.

Another advantage is that the shares traded on the IRS are priced in sterling, which means that investors are not subject to the usual charges associated with foreign exchange transactions. There's no need for the multi-currency accounts that often put people off investing internationally in the first place.

Setting up a US brokerage account

Investors who want to trade frequently in US stocks are likely to be better off with a fully-fledged US account. They will benefit from a much wider choice of investments and probably lower dealing charges. The only problem is that there are hundreds of brokers to choose from, such is the appetite for stock trading among US investors. Around 40 per cent of all US retail trades are now online.

Luckily there are online services that rate and review brokers to help you make a decision. One of the best is Gomez (www.gomez.com), a research consultancy. It provides 'scorecards' on a whole range of financial service providers, from internet banks

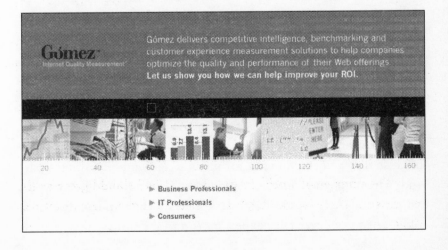

to brokers. Gomez is particularly useful because you can sort the brokers according to a number of different criteria. For example, you can see which is best suited to frequent traders or to long-term wealth builders. Gomez used to offer this service for UK brokers too, but has withdrawn it for commercial reasons.

Two execution-only US brokers I would recommend for serious traders are Ameritrade (www.ameritrade.com) and Datek (www.datek.com). They have very low dealing commissions and excellent research facilities. But bear in mind that wire transfers of funds from UK to US banks usually attract a charge of around $15.

Tax treatment

To invest in the US stocks you have to fill in a W-8BEN form – to prove that you are not a US resident. Otherwise you would have to pay a 30 per cent resident withholding tax on all dividends and interest. Once you have completed the form, tax on dividends and all interest is restricted to 15 per cent and is paid gross. It is up to you to declare the income from such shares in your tax return. If in doubt, seek advice from an accountant.

If you want to avoid this tax, look for stocks that do not pay dividends. These are usually fast-growing companies, perhaps in the high-tech sector and listed on Nasdaq, one of the major stock exchanges in the US. Foreign investors don't have to pay capital gains tax in the US, but you will be liable in the UK. Again, seek advice from your accountant or try the Inland Revenue's website (www.inlandrevenue.gov.uk).

US research resources

When you look at what is freely available to US investors you realise how far behind we are in this country. As a nation of investors, the US is far more sophisticated and experienced than we are, largely because they've been doing it for much longer and investing is part and parcel of the culture. Americans also have a Freedom of Information Act, which engenders a sense that information is a right, not a privilege. They expect more and get more in that respect.

Below are some useful websites for UK investors looking to enter the US market.

PUBLICATIONS

Business Week	www.businessweek.com
Chicago Sun-Times	www.suntimes.com
Forbes	www.forbes.com
Fortune	www.fortune.com

Kiplingers	kiplinger.com
New York Times	www.nytimes.com
San Jose Mercury News	www.sjmercury.com
Wall Street Journal (pay site)	www.wsj.com
Washington Post	www.washingtonpost.com

FINANCIAL NEWS

CNN Money   money.cnn.com

Bloomberg   www.bloomberg.com

Reuters   www.reuters.com

INVESTMENT RESEARCH

Motley Fool   www.fool.com

BigCharts   www.bigcharts.com

eSignal   www.esignal.com

WallStreetCity   www.wallstreetcity.com

Zacks Investment Research   www.zacks.com

Multex Investor   www.multexinvestor.com

Market Guide   www.marketguide.com

STOCK EXCHANGES
New York Stock Exchange   www.nyse.com
NASDAQ   www.nasdaq.com

Chicago Stock Exchange   www.chicagostockex.com

Setting up a European brokerage account

The UK investor looking to expand into European stocks is pretty well served these days by European brokers who have entered the UK market. Brokers like Comdirect and e-Cortal are blazing a trail others are sure to follow. There are also over 100 European stocks tradeable through the London Stock Exchange's International Retail Service, with more being added regularly, so as long as your UK broker offers international dealing you're unlikely to have to set up a Euro-denominated account. By far the best European brokerage ranking site is from BlueSky Ratings www.blueskyratings.com) – its analyses are extremely thorough and helpful.

But it has to be said that, so far, UK investors have shown little appetite for European stocks, save for a handful of well-known telecom companies, such as Nokia, Ericsson and Deutsche Telecom. There are far fewer dedicated European investment research sites than in the US, but the few are very good.

European research resources

Euromoney	www.euromoney.com
Euroland	www.euroland.com
Nasdaq Europe	www.nasdaqeurope.com
Wall Street Journal Europe (pay site)	www.europe.wsj.com
Financial Times	www.ft.com
Bloomberg	www.bloomberg.co.uk

6

Research and Trading Strategy

Introduction

So you've set up your brokerage account or fantasy portfolio on an investment-related website. Now you're ready to get your feet wet. But how do you decide what shares or other investments to commit your hard-earned to? And once you've decided what to buy, how do you know when to sell? How do you avoid the many pitfalls in the path of the online investor?

In this chapter we look at online resources you can use to help you decide what to invest in. We show you good sites for monitoring and analysing your investments and we discuss various trading strategies. But no one has all the answers. No one strategy is the right one, otherwise everyone would follow it and all investors would be rich. One strategy might be right in one set of circumstances, but when those circumstances change another strategy might be more suitable. Unfortunately, there are no easy solutions. But it is certainly true that the more effort you put into expanding your knowledge the better your investment decisions are likely to be.

There are many sources of investment ideas:

- your own experience of companies and their products

- press comment, tips and news

- investment information websites

- annual reports and accounts

- investor bulletin boards, newsgroups and chat rooms

- stock filtering websites

- technical analysis

Investors are blessed with an embarrassment of riches online. There are hundreds of investment-related websites, some concentrating on trading strategies, others on providing fundamental financial data and tools to help investors analyse that data. There is something for everyone.

Basic Price and Chart Data

Share prices are obviously important to online investors – they indicate whether you are making profits or losses. The ability to see their movements visually in the form of charts or graphs is also important. Your online broker will be the first place you'll look for price data. Simply find out the code of the company you're interested in and search. But most brokers supply share prices that are delayed by fifteen to twenty minutes since stock exchanges tend to charge for live price feeds. You can usually pay more to receive live prices continually streamed to your PC and you are obviously given a live share price when you want to buy or sell.

Historic price data is also important to investors because it helps to put current price levels into perspective. Good charting facilities that include the ability to compare share price performance against other stocks or benchmark indices are essential. Again, your broker should be able to provide this, unless you've opted for one of the no-frills discount brokers. Many provide e-mail alert services to

PC and mobile devices so that you can keep up to date with price movements even when you're away from your desk or actually doing your day job for a change!

There are plenty of non-broker sites that provide delayed and real-time prices as well as other useful indicators, such as trade volume, intra-day price graphs and percentage price changes on the day. For most investors who trade only a few times a year, real-time prices are obviously not that important. But they are essential for the frequent trader looking to benefit from intra-day price movements.

Some useful websites:

Stockpoint   http://investor.stockpoint.com
Teletext   www.teletext.co.uk

Teletext > Home

—— Jan 8 2002 ————————

Welcome

TODAY ON THE SITE

Carey: Planning to quit
The Archbishop of Canterbury is planning his retirement - but who will take up the mantle of head of the Church of England?

Updata	www.updata.co.uk
Free Real Time (US)	www.freerealtime.com
European Investor	www.europeaninvestor.com
UK Share Net	www.uksharenet.co.uk
The Sharepage	www.thesharepage.com
BigCharts	www.bigcharts.com
FTMarketWatch	www.ftmarketwatch.com

Stock Exchanges

Stock exchange websites are also a useful – and sometimes overlooked – source of price data and company news. Here's a list of the main ones:

LONDON STOCK EXCHANGE
www.londonstockexchange.com

The LSE's site has rapidly improved over the last year or so, with far more attention paid to useful services for the private investor, including data on techMARK and Alternative Investment Market companies, plus new investments, such as Exchange Traded Funds.

OFEX   www.ofex.com

Ofex is the unregulated market for very small companies run by market maker J. P. Jenkins. As yet you can't invest online in Ofex-

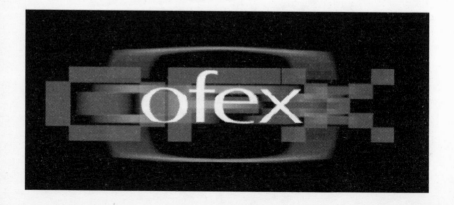

listed companies, you have to deal by phone. But interest has been growing in the market as wily investors look for the next major growth stock. Successful Ofex companies will often seek a listing on the bigger Alternative Investment Market or the main market, so speculative investors try to spot them when they're still tiny, in the hope of making a spectacular return later. The site lists share prices and company financial results. If interest continues to rise, Ofex should become more automated, enabling its information to be shown on broker and investment information websites.

NASDAQ www.nasdaq.com

The Nasdaq has become synonymous with high-tech companies and the dot.com bubble. But it has led the way in providing excellent research resources for investors, including analyst research, company reports and fundamentals.

NEW YORK STOCK EXCHANGE www.nyse.com

This is a neatly designed site from the US's biggest exchange with ticker-tape-style share prices constantly moving across your screen.

Fundamental data

The most straightforward approach to investing is the one that takes a good hard look at companies' businesses – their profits, cash flow and earnings potential. After all, if a company is making something that is popular, has lots of cash in the bank and has been increasing its turnover and profits year in year out, it would seem like a sure-fire winner. To some extent that is true. But if only it were that simple.

Everyone else may have come to the same conclusion as you and decided to invest in this company. As we know, increased demand for something pushes up the price. At some point that company's share price will rise so high that it bears little relation to its actual or potential earnings. It will have become overvalued. Now, the share price could continue rising as more and more investors jump on the bandwagon, but it could equally fall rapidly as institutional investors decide that the current share price is unsustainable, take their profits and move on.

The classic mistake that many private investors make is to dive in just before this happens. They assume that because a share price has been rising for some time it will continue to rise. It won't if the market believes that company has become overvalued. And this is why it is essential for investors to keep abreast of companies' fundamental financial data. Basic indicators, such as the price/earnings ratio and earnings per share, are only the tip of the iceberg.

COMPANY REPORTS AND ANALYST RESEARCH

The best way to get a feel for a company and its business is to read its annual report and accounts, and in-depth research conducted by institutional stockbrokers. The more you know about a company you're thinking of investing in the more confident you will be when you come to commit your cash. What the chairman and chief executive say about the company's trading record and prospects can be extremely important.

You'll want to look at how the company's sales are growing, how fast earnings per share are growing, how much debt the company is having to service and the cashflow situation. If the company is a young technology business, how soon does it expect to reach profitability and does it have enough cash in the bank to last until it does? For useful explanations of these indicators and how they should be used to arrive at investment decisions, visit some of the investment sites recommended in Chapter 3.

If you are already a shareholder you are entitled to the report and accounts anyway, but if you're not, you can order reports and accounts easily online from a number of sites:

Digital Look   www.digital-look.com

Hoovers   **www.hoovers.com**

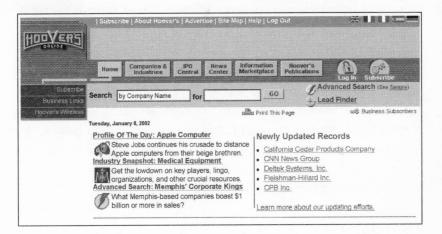

Corporate Reports   **www.corpreports.co.uk**
FT.com   **www.ft.com**

ProShare   **www.proshare.org**
EDGAR (US)   **www.sec.gov/edgar.shtml**

If you don't want to read the full report you can see company financial snapshots and read analyst research. The added advantage of such research is that brokers make 'buy', 'sell' or 'hold' recommendations for their clients. This advice used to be reserved solely for high-paying institutions but is now freely available to private investors. It is yet another example of how much more informed private investors can be these days. Obviously those institutional clients get to see the research and act upon it before we do. That's what they pay large sums of money for. This means that the share price might have been affected before we get to see the recommendation. Even so it doesn't necessarily negate the usefulness of such research reports. They tell us a lot about the company, its peers in the sector, and the general market conditions.

Again, good online brokers will provide analyst research and fundamental company data for investors, but here are some alternative providers (some free, some subscription):

Hemmington Scott	www.hemscott.net
Multex Investor	www.multexinvestor.com
Digital Look	www.digitallook.com
Merrill Lynch HSBC	www.mlhsbc.co.uk
Citywire	www.citywire.co.uk
Company REFS	www.companyrefs.com

Filtering sites

There are so many stocks to choose from that sites which help narrow down your choice are welcome. Some investment sites can filter stocks according to a wide range of criteria. For example, you may be interested in companies with high earnings growth, low p/e ratios and whose directors have been buying the shares. These sites are pretty good at explaining the reasons why such financial indicators are considered important.

As usual, US investors are better served than UK investors, but here's a list of useful filtering sites that can help you with your stock selection:

Stockpoint	www.stockpoint.com
Digital Look	www.digitallook.com
Sharescope (software)	www.sharescope.co.uk
WallStreetCity (US)	www.wallstreetcity.com
Zacks (US)	www.zacks.com

Automated help?

In the US brokers are trying to develop sophisticated online stock and fund selection tools that will help investors choose the right investments. For example, the investor may fill in a questionnaire asking about his or her age, financial situation and tolerance of risk. The broker's automated system will then throw up some shares or funds it deems suitable. Investment purists hate this idea, however, because it breaks one of the cardinal rules of investing: do your own research. The more you learn about investing, through reading and observing, the more likely it is you will make good investment decisions. Automated systems that make the decisions for you could hinder this process of self-education. The online investor should never be totally reliant on someone else's research or hunches.

Anyway, we're some way away from that level of service in the UK. So if you feel you need more help deciding what to buy and what strategy to adopt, maybe you should seek independent advice or go to an advisory broker.

Basic Trading Strategies Explained

What are your investment goals?

One of the most important first steps to take is deciding what your investment goals are. Putting it bluntly, do you want to take big risks to make a million fast, or are you happy to take the long-term, incremental approach to building wealth? Do you have sufficient funds to adopt both strategies, apportioning some of your capital to the long term and some to short-term speculation?

The answers to these questions depend largely on your personality and how much time you are able or prepared to devote to managing your investments. Not everyone is happy taking risks and not everyone is in a position to lose much money (in which case maybe you shouldn't be contemplating direct equity investment at all, but start off with safer collective investments, such as unit trusts and open-ended investment companies).

The internet makes share dealing very quick and easy. This can be both a blessing and a curse. It can tempt investors to dabble with their long-term investments when they should just leave well alone. And if you're unclear about your investment strategy, the wrong decisions are likely to follow. You could end up fiddling with your long-term portfolio while ignoring the 'buy' and 'sell' signals in your short-term, speculative portfolio. That way leads to financial disaster.

Diversity is key

A basic investment principle is that if you put all your eggs in one basket, the chances of coming a cropper are greatly increased. Spreading your cash between several companies can reduce this risk. This process of diversification can be as wide as you like. For example, if your entire portfolio consists of technology and biotechnology companies, this would be considered very high risk. It would be safer to diversify into different sectors, such as food, or banks. These are thought of as relatively safe, although perhaps less likely to produce rocketing returns.

As your portfolio grows and you put more money into it, you might decide that concentrating on the UK market alone is putting all your eggs in one basket on a global scale. You could diversify your portfolio even further by investing in stocks in the US, European or Far Eastern markets. We saw in Chapter Four how a growing number of UK brokers will let you do this now. And if you buy shares in a UK-listed international investment trust or Exchange Traded Fund (see Chapter 7) you get exposure to global markets without having to spend more on international dealing costs.

All this is about spreading risk. Understanding the nature of risk is essential to good investing. A small, newly formed company with a top-notch product could have amazing potential. You might make thousands if it took off. You might equally lose everything if the fledgling company stumbles along the way, as so many do. Some people are prepared to take high risks in the hope of high returns. Others are happy to take the long, slow road to wealth creation. As world-famous investor Warren Buffett said: 'It is better to be certain of a good result than hopeful of a great one.'

Setting stop-losses

Experienced investors all say that these two practices are vital. Setting a stop-loss means deciding at what point you sell if the share price falls by 10 per cent, say. The idea is that if a share price is falling by that much, there must be a reason for it. Better to cut your losses now and then buy the shares again at a later date when they seem to be established on an upward trend once more. This way you protect your capital and pick up far more shares for the same money.

Not all shares do recover. Companies do go bust. All investors occasionally pick a dud. So it makes no sense to hang on to shares that are falling in value – although sticking rigidly to stop-losses is one of the hardest disciplines for investors. But it can be counter-productive if you set your stop loss too tight. For example, a particularly volatile share might fluctuate by plus or minus 5 per cent on a regular basis. If you constantly sell when the price hits your stop-loss you'll end up eating away your capital through dealing charges and the bid-offer spread.

Even long-term investors should set stop-losses, just in case the company doesn't recover, but perhaps they could be more generous in the level they set them at. Make the most of e-mail-alert services to warn you if some of your shares hit your stop-losses. That way you won't get caught out by sudden drops caused by a profit warning, say.

Taking profits

Taking profits regularly is a good discipline, because until the money is in the bank any profit is just notional. It could easily disappear again on some piece of bad corporate news. The problem is that when shares are rising, we get greedy. We think they'll go on rising for ever and we're loath to sell for fear of missing out on even more. Of course, shares don't often carry on rising for ever. You have to decide what level of profit you'd be happy with and try not to be too greedy.

One strategy is to hedge your bets, sell half your holding and leave the rest, just in case they do carry on rising. It is very common to hear investors regretting that they sold out too soon and could have made a lot of money if they'd held on. It is equally common to hear investors regretting that they didn't sell when the share price was sky-high after it has plummeted. The old investment saying 'Nobody ever went broke taking a profit' is worth remembering.

Investment is a lot about timing. But people can get carried away trying to predict when share prices are at the very bottom or the very top. It's better to cut your losses and take your profits when you can and 'leave a little for the other guy'.

Day trading

Buying and selling shares during the day in the hope of making a quick profit from the daily fluctuations in share prices is the high-adrenalin end of the investment game. Most day traders don't hold shares overnight. 'Real-time' internet share dealing has driven growth in day trading because it has made it much easier for private investors to react quickly to price movements. But it is a high-risk activity. Most investors end up losing money because the dealing charges they pay per trade wipe out the profits they make. The bid-offer spread – the difference between the price at which you can buy or sell a share – also means that the shares have to perform strongly just to break even. On top of these factors, 0.5 per cent stamp duty on all share purchases in the UK makes day trading even more expensive. Unless you have large sums to invest, a broker with cheap, flat-rate dealing commissions and an uncanny ability to pick winners consistently, you are almost guaranteed to lose money.

Selling short

Some astute investors manage to make money even when markets are falling. They sell short, which means they sell shares they don't own yet. They hope that the share price will fall before they have to settle the contract and deliver the shares. They then pocket the difference between the two prices. It's a risky practice and one best avoided by nearly all novice investors. Most UK online brokers don't allow it anyway.

Advanced Investment Strategies

Value investing

Value investors are those who believe that the fundamentals of a company's business are most important – how much cash is in the bank, how fast its profits are growing, and so on. They believe that this is the only basis on which to buy shares. They look closely at all the financial data, the potential future earnings, and decide whether the company is undervalued or overvalued compared with other companies in the same sector. The comparison will suggest a buying or a selling opportunity.

Sometimes one company's share price can fall for no other reason than that a similar company's share price fell, even when there was no fundamental reason why this should happen. Fundamental investors will see this as a buying opportunity because the market has temporarily failed to value the company correctly.

But there are lots of theories about the weighting you give to each fundamental indicator. For example, some believe companies with high debt should be avoided altogether. Others think that these borrowings will help the company to grow faster. One investor may only be interested in companies whose dividends have been growing by a certain percentage each year, another may consider earnings-per-share growth to be more important.

It isn't in the remit of this book to recommend one investment theory over another – they all have their merits – but you can find plenty of explanations of the different theories on investor websites such as Motley Fool (www.fool.co.uk), Ample Interactive Investor (www.ample.com) and FT Investor (www.ft.com/investor).

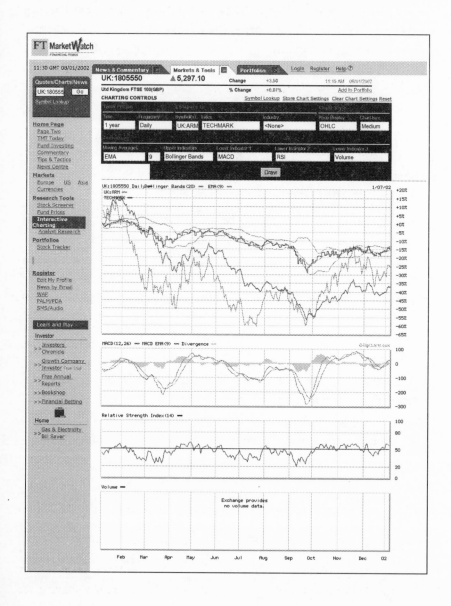

Technical analysis

Another school of thought believes that company fundamentals have little to do with share prices and that sentiment, fear and greed have more to do with the behaviour of stock markets. There is something to be said for this. The phrase 'The trend is your friend' certainly applies. This means that if the markets are heading strongly in one direction, no piece of good or bad news from one company will have any effect. The fundamentals of the company may still be good, but the share price will fall nonetheless.

This approach is called 'technical analysis' and is mostly associated with short-term trading. It becomes controversial when its proponents claim absolute powers of prediction just through studying graphs and charts. They look at a number of different measures of share price performance – some of which are described below – trying to discern patterns in the behaviour of that particular share. If it is taken too far it can seem equivalent to reading tea leaves, but shares can and do follow a rough pattern of behaviour.

For example, a share may be very volatile, rising and falling with dizzying frequency. But a look at the price performance chart might reveal that the overall direction is still upwards and that the degree of volatility is within a predictable range. This can tell investors that if a share price has fallen by a set amount already, and the fundamentals of the stock haven't changed, it is unlikely to fall much further, suggesting a buying opportunity.

In short, technical analysis is just a way to find out when to buy low and sell high. Here are some of the most common indicators:

Trendlines – straight lines drawn on a share price graph joining successive price lows or highs to establish an upwards or downwards trend. It is a way of ignoring the short-term volatility of a stock to ascertain its general movement.
Support and resistance lines – lines showing the general level at which a share price hasn't fallen below or risen above. It can show whether it is a good time to buy or sell. For instance, if a share price is very close to or below its established support level it could be a good time to buy, provided nothing has changed about the

fundamentals of the company or the general economic outlook. Vice versa if the price is close to its resistance level. If it breaks through the resistance level, investors often use that as a signal to buy.

Moving averages – lines plotted by taking the average share price over the last X days. It is common to combine a long-moving average – 200-day – with a shorter-moving average – 30-day. The points where the two lines intersect are taken to be buy or sell signals.

Momentum indicators – there are several different types of momentum indicator but they all do much the same thing, which is to assess whether the enthusiasm for a particular share is waxing or waning. Investors tend to move in herds – where one leads the others follow. So if there has been a broker recommendation on a stock or some positive press comment, say, a load of investors may pile into that stock and continue to do so. There is momentum behind the investor sentiment. That will eventually slow down, and momentum indicators, such as stochastic and moving average convergence/ divergence, aim to pinpoint this process.

Bollinger bands – lines plotted at certain standard deviations above and below moving share price averages. They are often used to identify imminent price movements either up or down when the band narrows.

Many books have been written about technical analysis and we don't have room to explore the jargon-filled world completely. Instead, here are some useful online resources to get you started:

Chartman	www.chartman.co.uk
ClearStation	www.clearstation.com
Equis	www.equis.com
BigCharts	www.bigcharts.com
E*Trade	www.etrade.co.uk
Decision Point	www.decisionpoint.com
Stockcharts	www.stockcharts.com
FTMarketwatch	www.ftmarketwatch.com
Motley Fool	www.fool.co.uk/mechanicalhome.htm

CHAPTER 7

Other Investments

Introduction

Equities are not the only investments you can buy and sell online –
which is probably just as well, given the volatility of the global
markets during 2001. In this chapter we take a look at the whole
range of alternative online investments, from options to self-invested
personal pensions. But we concentrate on investment funds – unit
trusts and open-ended investment companies.

In many ways UK investors are much more comfortable with
this type of investment. They involve pooled funds and lots of
underlying companies, helping to spread risk. We have traditionally
been rather risk averse in our investment decisions. Yes, racy new
investments, such as contracts for difference (CFDs) and spread-
betting have entered the scene, but the money these forms of
investment attract will never rival the £250 billion investors have
piled into Personal Equity Plans and Individual Savings Accounts
over the years.

Funds Online

Funds have taken longer than equities to get online because they are less time-sensitive investments. Their prices are updated just once a day and investors usually buy for the long term. The fast-paced world of the internet has seemed irrelevant. For this reason we still don't have electronic settlement of funds, as we do with most equities. Big fund management companies with billions of pounds under management still write cheques to banks and each other. It's a curiously old-fashioned world.

All that is changing, thanks to the internet and the introduction of 'fund supermarkets'. Launched in late 1999 and throughout 2000, fund supermarkets have firmly gripped the imagination of the fund management industry in the UK. A one-stop-shop trading platform enabling investors to buy funds from several management companies, but receive consolidated statements within or outside an Individual Savings Account wrapper, a fund supermarket is a significant new distribution channel that threatens to shake up the industry.

The concept first originated in the US in the early 1990s, pioneered by discount stockbroker Charles Schwab and Fidelity Investments, the world's largest fund manager. It has since transformed the industry and made the idea of 'no-load' funds – no initial charge – commonplace.

According to Datamonitor, the research consultancy, the UK fund supermarket industry is experiencing significant competitive pressures already as the number of new players entering the market has increased. There are around sixteen companies in the fund supermarket industry now with this figure expected to rise to twenty by the end of 2001. At the time of writing, Legal & General, Norwich Union and J.P. Morgan Fleming were in the process of joining in.

But Datamonitor believes the UK market cannot sustain so many companies. Mergers and acquisitions are inevitable. We've already seen Ample, AMP's fund supermarket, merge with Interactive Investor International, the personal finance website and fund intermediary. More will follow.

Some experts speculate that supermarkets spell doom for the traditional independent financial adviser (IFA). Others have thought that they signal an age of ever-increasing profit margin pressure on fund providers as the supermarkets become more powerful, eventually dictating business terms. Price and performance transparency on the web will also increase the pressure on active fund managers to justify annual management charges in the light of cheap, passively managed index-tracking funds.

What does this mean for the online investor? More choice, greater convenience and lower prices, basically. Competition is always good from the consumer's point of view. But IFAs aren't likely to disappear overnight. People will always need advice and IFAs are still the main way funds are sold in this country. This will remain the case for some time.

Not all fund supermarkets are the same

In the strict sense a fund supermarket is a company that offers a wide range of funds from a broad selection of fund managers, and the ability to buy and sell those funds online. Investors should be able to manage their portfolios online, carry out fund performance research and have their accounts handled by the fund supermarket direct.

But some websites call themselves fund supermarkets when all they are doing is providing links to fund manager websites. Some let you invest inside or outside an ISA, others are ISA-only. Some process your online application almost instantaneously thanks to direct electronic links with fund managers, others take longer because they're not fully automated yet. Some sell direct to private investors, others only supply their services to intermediaries.

What's so good about fund supermarkets?

Fund providers have a new, more efficient distribution channel for their funds. As all our buy and sell orders are lumped together – aggregated to use the jargon – and executed within the supermarket's nominee account, the fund provider saves time and money by not having to service lots and lots of separate applications. And as the supermarket handles the customer relationship, the provider no longer has to worry about answering valuation queries, sending out reports and accounts, dividend distribution statements and so on. The administrative savings have been estimated to be anything up to 30 per cent.

The fund provider can theoretically spend fewer resources on marketing and promotion, relying more on the supermarket to do that. These savings can be passed on to the investor in the form of lower initial and annual management charges.

IFAs can also benefit from a supermarket's ability to handle customer data and provide a central transactional platform. Rather than having to apply separately to each fund provider, an IFA can fill in one form, either offline or online, and transact far more efficiently. A supermarket can take away much of the administrative burden associated with funds investment, freeing up time for the IFA to concentrate on building relationships with clients and offering more lucrative wealth management services.

For private investors four advantages are clear:

CONVENIENCE

It is much easier for an investor to research and choose funds, fill in one application form and pay online, all in one place. Before, the investor would have had to request a paper application form by phone or by post, or filled it in online, for each different fund provider. Such a lengthy and time-consuming process would not have endeared the whole business of investing in funds to the investor. The general rule in financial services is that if you make it easier for people to do, they're more likely to do it. Giving a debit card number, bank account details and maybe a National Insurance Number is all very straightforward and easy for the investor. It saves time. Having a consolidated valuation statement is also useful.

Cost

Most inexperienced investors probably do not realise that if they respond to a fund provider's advert in a newspaper and invest direct, they usually pay a much higher initial charge than if they had gone through a discount broker or fund supermarket. It cannot be long before this knowledge becomes widespread. Most supermarkets negotiate full or partial discounting of the initial charge, making it much more cost-effective for investors, especially the wealthy, to invest this way. Instead of the usual 4–6 per cent initial charge, you typically pay 0–1.5 per cent through a fund supermarket.

Greater choice

Sophisticated investors will know how to make the most of online analytical tools, giving a whole range of performance and risk-assessment data. The results of their searches may well lead them to different providers from those normally found advertising in newspapers and being continually plugged in articles. A fund supermarket supplies this type of investor with easy access to a wider choice of funds, provided, of course, the supermarket is willing to put breadth of choice above brand recognition in its offering.

Familiarity

Novice investors are unlikely to have heard of most fund managers, even the leading lights. As the industry reaches out to the mass market, new investors are likely to migrate to brands they know and trust. Inexperienced investors, without the time or inclination to carry out research and select their own funds, will happily rely on a recognised brand name to do it for them. This is why pre-packaged themed ISAs from the likes of Egg are proving popular.

Are there any disadvantages?

The only real disadvantage for retail investors is if the choice of funds is restricted by the fund supermarket. There is no guarantee that a supermarket will offer all the funds that boast the most consistent performance with the lowest volatility. Fund super-markets may be tempted to go for the big brands only, sacrificing performance on the altar of popularity.

The main contenders

Although there are lots of fund supermarkets around now, there are some clear leaders in the field. These are my favourites that are directly accessible to online investors:

FIDELITY FUNDSNETWORK (www.fundsnetwork.co.uk)

Fidelity's FundsNetwork is the leading contender in the supermarket stakes. It is open to the public and intermediaries alike, combining an excellent choice of funds – 560 from thirty-seven leading fund managers – with cutting-edge technology to make your online application process as easy as possible. You can invest inside or outside an ISA, choose from its own range of funds, and compare and contrast fund performance using Standard & Poor's Micropal

ratings. Its educational content is very useful, too. The site has also been redesigned to make it more easily digestible. Typical initial charges are 1.25 per cent.

EGG FUND SUPERMARKET (www.egg.com)

Egg's site is refreshingly simple in design and offers a reasonable choice of funds. I particularly like its pre-packaged ISAs that include funds from different managers based on investment themes, such as technology or UK growth. These should appeal to investors without the time or inclination to carry out exhaustive research. Performance data and ratings are supplied by Reuters Lipper and Standard & Poor's Micropal for those investors who like carrying out their own research.

CHARCOLONLINE (www.charcolonline.co.uk)

Charcolonline, the online financial services arm of Bradford & Bingley, uses FundsHub to power its supermarket. It was the first

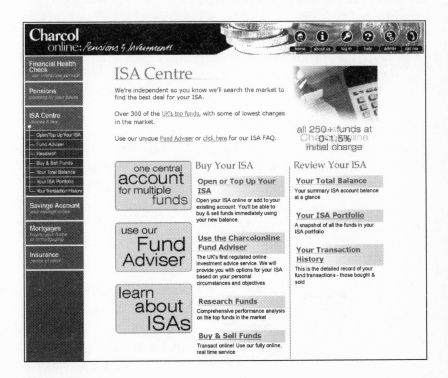

intermediary to offer specific fund recommendations through is fully automated online advice system. The Q&A takes twenty minutes to complete, and comes up with specific fund recommendations based on your risk tolerance and investment objectives. There are 250 funds from twenty-four fund managers on its panel, but there's no guarantee that its recommendations will be the best-performing funds. The site is very well designed and good telephone support is a bonus.

AMPLE (www.ample.com)

Ample, owned by AMP, the Australian banking giant, realises that all investors are different. You can do your own research, use its fund selector tool to narrow down the choice, or simply hand over your cash and let them choose the funds for you. It offers over 400 funds from twenty-four managers. There are plenty of performance and news resources to help choose and monitor their funds.

FUNDSDIRECT (www.fundsdirect.co.uk)

FundsDirect is notable for its amazing choice of 1500 funds that you can buy online inside or outside an ISA wrapper. Its fund selector tool is very sophisticated, allowing investors to hone down their searches to funds with specific characteristics, such as risk rating and investment sector.

Buying funds through brokers

Quite a few brokers now offer funds through their share-dealing sites, but watch out for dealing and administration charges on self-select ISAs. Unless you particularly like having all your investments under the same roof, you may be better off going to a fund super-market or specialist intermediary.

The leading stockbrokers selling funds are:

E*Trade	www.etrade.co.uk
Charles Schwab	www.schwab-europe.com
Barclays Stockbrokers	www.barclays-stockbrokers.co.uk
T. D. Waterhouse	www.tdwaterhouse.co.uk

Buying funds through intermediaries

The main disadvantage of buying funds through a fund supermarket is that you don't get advice (Charcolonline excepted). They provide research tools for you, but some investors need more hand holding than that. This is why IFAs are also worth checking out. You can usually opt for an execution-only service or one that includes advice. Sometimes the advice is even free.

My favourites are:

BEST INVESTMENT (**www.bestinvest.co.uk**)

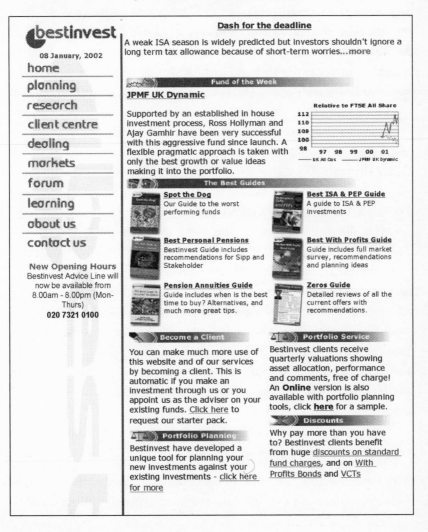

bestinvest

08 January, 2002

home

planning

research

client centre

dealing

markets

forum

learning

about us

contact us

New Opening Hours
Bestinvest Advice Line will
now be available from
8.00am - 8.00pm (Mon-
Thurs)
020 7321 0100

Dash for the deadline

A weak ISA season is widely predicted but investors shouldn't ignore a long term tax allowance because of short-term worries...more

Fund of the Week

JPMF UK Dynamic

Supported by an established in house investment process, Ross Hollyman and Ajay Gamhir have been very successful with this aggressive fund since launch. A flexible pragmatic approach is taken with only the best growth or value ideas making it into the portfolio.

Relative to FTSE All Share
112 110 108 100 98 — 97 98 99 00 01
UK All Cos — JPMF UK Dynamic

The Best Guides

Spot the Dog
Our Guide to the worst performing funds

Best Personal Pensions
Bestinvest Guide includes recommendations for Sipp and Stakeholder

Pension Annuities Guide
Guide includes when is the best time to buy? Alternatives, and much more great tips.

Best ISA & PEP Guide
A guide to ISA & PEP investments

Best With Profits Guide
Guide includes full market survey, recommendations and planning ideas

Zeros Guide
Detailed reviews of all the current offers with recommendations.

Become a Client

You can make much more use of this website and of our services by becoming a client. This is automatic if you make an investment through us or you appoint us as the adviser on your existing funds. Click here to request our starter pack.

Portfolio Planning

Bestinvest have developed a unique tool for planning your new investments against your existing investments - click here for more

Portfolio Service

Bestinvest clients receive quarterly valuations showing asset allocation, performance and comments, free of charge! An **Online** version is also available with portfolio planning tools, click **here** for a sample.

Discounts

Why pay more than you have to? Bestinvest clients benefit from huge discounts on standard fund charges, and on With Profits Bonds and VCTs

An investment specialist that uses both FundsNetwork and another supermarket called Cofunds. It discounts a lot of its commission from fund providers to provide investors with very low initial charges, often better than the supermarkets themselves offer. There are fund recommendations, newsletters and research resources at your disposal.

AISA Direct (www.aisa.co.uk)

In December 2001 AISA Direct launched its own fund supermarket in conjunction with Skandia Life, the insurance giant that pioneered the concept of multi-fund PEPs. Skandia deals exclusively with intermediaries. Around 200 funds are available through the service. AISA forecast the current market downturn and was dissuading clients from investing in equities funds back in March 2001, so it seems to know its onions. The site is packed with general investment guides and analysis, plus model portfolios to suit different types of investor. You can assess your own tolerance to risk using an online Q&A and receive sizeable discounts on initial charges if you invest online through AISA.

Torquil Clark (www.tqonline.co.uk)

Another discount adviser in the same mould as Best Investment, Torquil Clark also features model portfolios containing suggested fund combinations to suit different investors. For example, retired investors may need income from their investments, whereas young people can afford to look for long-term growth and perhaps take more risk. Torquil has also linked up with Fidelity FundsNetwork. You can buy discounted ISAs online using your debit card. You can also find general advice on the site, but if you want one-to-one advice you have to pay fees or commission depending on the level of service you need.

Research and monitoring services

Watching PEP and ISA investments being decimated in these volatile markets is alarming enough for investors, especially those close to retirement. Trying to decide what to do about it can be equally stressful. Do you sit tight, switch to a more defensive fund, or bail out altogether?

Even before the terrorist attacks of 11 September 2001 in the US, things weren't looking too rosy for investment funds. In August, gross industry sales were down 22 per cent compared with a year ago, according to the Association of Unit Trusts and Investment Funds, and total funds under management now stand at around £230 billion, compared with £280 billion a year ago. PricewaterhouseCoopers, the consultancy, predicts that a worrying third of UK fund managers will have suffered losses in 2001.

In this kind of climate it is all the more important to find the managers who are best equipped to cope and to monitor your investments closely. Some funds may never recover the loss they have made. It's a brutal fact that many investors fail to come to terms with.

Fortunately, the quality of fund research sites has improved markedly over the last couple of years. The performance data now freely available online is staggering. We've already mentioned the fund supermarkets, brokers and intermediaries who all provide fund research of one sort or another. But here are a few more useful sites to help you find the right funds to suit your investment objectives.

AMPLE INTERACTIVE INVESTOR (www.ample.com)

This personal finance portal now owned by AMP, the Australian banking and insurance giant, has a useful investment funds section that compares 400 funds from thirty fund managers. As well as the usual ability to analyse fund performance, you can also ring up for personal financial advice from a Towry Law independent financial adviser. Calls cost 75p per minute. The site features an 'ISA Assistant' to help you assess your risk tolerance and the type of funds best suited to you. Although there isn't much news or strategic advice on the site, you can at least swap views with fellow investors on the bulletin board.

STANDARD & POOR'S FUNDS-SP (www.funds-sp.co.uk)

The dedicated funds site from one of the world's most respected financial data providers offers a bewildering amount of information on around 40,000 mutual funds worldwide. Not only do you get a fact sheet giving details of the particular fund management group and its charges, you also get table after table of performance data, showing how the funds have performed over various time periods compared with others. There's even analysis of how consistent the fund's performance has been. This is especially useful since fund managers can often give a misleading impression of their worth by highlighting the one or two years of stellar growth, while failing to put these in the context of a dismal overall track record. It's hard to see how you need any other site.

MORNINGSTAR (www.morningstar.co.uk)

The UK site of this well-known US performance data provider is also jam-packed with useful comparative information to help you pick the best of the crop. Bear in mind, though, that none of these performance analysis sites can predict the future. A fantastic performance to date is no guarantee of continued excellence. But what such sites can do well is give investors a stronger sense of a fund manager's reliability over the long term. Consistency of performance is an important factor when choosing funds, and ratings of the kind that Morningstar and S&P provide are very helpful.

TRUSTNET (www.trustnet.com)

As well as monitoring your fund portfolio on this site, you can really get to grips with the minutiae of the funds you've invested in or are planning to invest in. TrustNet provides detailed tabular data on most funds, which includes information about the management teams and the biggest constituent investments made by the fund. This is useful to prevent you duplicating investments. If your chosen fund already invests in Cisco, for example, there may be little point in buying shares as well in that company.

CITYWIRE (www.citywire.co.uk)

This investment news provider also offers a very useful service that tracks the performance of individual fund managers. A fund's performance can often dip following the departure of a talented manager, so now investors can make sure they follow the talent that makes the decisions and not the management company's brand.

Investing in funds direct

When the Government introduced Individual Savings Accounts in April 1999 there was an important concession that allowed investors to open accounts and make deposits online without the need for a written signature. Fidelity Investments jumped on the chance and led the charge to allow investors to apply for funds and make deposits into them online.

But other fund managers were lamentably slow following suit. They are gradually catching up, although many are still in two minds about the benefits of selling direct online when they have a network of IFAs that does their selling for them. Some IFAs are also very unhappy when product providers go direct to the public as it cuts them out of the picture.

But if this is what investors want and expect, this is what fund managers should provide. At the very least we should be able to monitor our funds online at the manager's site, rather than going to some other investment site. For a full list of investment management company websites go to the Association of Unit Trust and Investment Companies (AUTIF) website (www.investmentfunds.org.uk).

EXCHANGE TRADED FUNDS (ETFs)

Exchange Traded Funds are a hybrid investment – half share, half fund. Originating in the US – where else? – they are types of passive tracker funds following indices of various kinds. This means you can gain access to a very wide cross-section of companies in just one investment. There are many varieties, some tracking particular stock market sectors, such as healthcare, for example, others that will track the main index of a foreign market.

The innovative part is that they can be bought and sold throughout the trading day just like ordinary shares. This allows investors to be far more responsive to price movements and gain exposure to different sectors at a much lower cost than conventional funds. US investors can also buy them on margin, which means effectively borrowing money from the broker to buy a far larger number of shares. This can have the effect of magnifying your gains (and losses) drastically. They can also be 'sold short', which means selling shares you don't yet own in the hope that the price has fallen by the time you have to honour the contract (see Chapter 6).

The UK's first ETFs began trading on the London Stock Exchange in early 2001 – seven years after the US. The London Stock Exchange set up extraMARK to host ETFs and other innovative investments. If you go to the LSE website (www.londonstockexchange.com) and click on the extraMARK link you can view a list of all the ETFs currently available to UK investors and see their prices (delayed by fifteen minutes).

The first UK ETF was launched by a company called iShares and tracks the FTSE 100, the UK's main index. Now there are around fifteen ETFs tracking general and sector-specific indices from iShares, Bloomberg and Dow Jones.

The sector-specific funds give you instant access to an international basket of companies from a particular industry. For example, the iShares iBloomberg Parmaceutical Fund contains around thirty major pharmaceutical companies from the UK, Denmark, France, Switzerland and Germany. Adding a few of these shares to your portfolio gives you instant diversification.

But perhaps the biggest attraction of ETFs is their low cost. The annual management charge is often less than 0.5 per cent. This compares favourably with the average for conventional index funds, which is between 0.5 per cent and 1 per cent on average. This pricing regime has been made possible because ETFs tend not to carry front- or back-end charges, or sales commissions. They are also held in non-certificated form, which cuts down on administration costs.

We have some way to go before we match the extremely low costs enjoyed in the States, however. Their economies of scale and massive retail and institutional investment markets allow some managers to charge annual management fees of less than 0.2 per cent. As the market grows in the UK – and there's every likelihood that it will as investors wise up to the many advantages of ETFs – our charges may come down too.

Most online brokers, including major names, such as E*Trade, Charles Schwab and DLJ Direct, have incorporated ETFs into their services. Have a look at the iShares (www.ishares.net) website for more information about ETFs and a list of online brokers who offer them.

Futures and Options

FUTURES

Futures are legally binding contracts where one party agrees to deliver and the other to accept a certain commodity at a pre-agreed time, place and price. They are traded via exchanges such as LIFFE – the London International Financial Futures and Options Exchange (www.liffe.com). An investor is said to be 'long' on a futures contract if he has agreed to accept delivery of the commodity, 'short' if he has agreed to deliver. The price is derived from the price of the underlying asset – hence the term 'derivatives'.

They are one of the oldest forms of security devised by farmers looking to guarantee payment for their harvests. This is why futures are traditionally associated with commodities, such as gold, oil, coffee and wheat. In fact, the vast majority of futures contracts are not held until delivery but 'closed' before then. This means an equal and opposite contract is made to cancel out your legally binding obligations. Most people who speculate in futures care not one jot for the underlying asset.

Nowadays you can speculate on the future movement of stock market indices using such contracts. For each point an index moves you make or lose £X or $X, depending on the nature of the contract.

Futures are usually bought on margin. This means you only pay a fraction of the contract's real value. So if a futures contract was worth £20,000, you might only pay £2000 to buy it. If that contract moved just 5 per cent it would have a £1000 (50 per cent) effect on your initial investment.

This effect is called 'leverage' and is the main reason why futures are scary and exciting at the same time. If the future moves aggressively against you, you can lose a lot of money very quickly. And you are legally bound to pay up what you owe. This extra cash you need to cough up is called 'variation margin' as opposed to the 'initial margin' – the money you put up initially.

Bear in mind that these are the securities that Nic Leeson managed to bring down Barings Bank with!

OPTIONS

Options are also derivatives where you have the right, but not the obligation, to buy or sell a certain commodity at a pre-agreed price at a set time in the future. There are two types of option: a call option and put option. A call option is the right to buy, a put option is the right to sell. In the UK equity options relate to the right to buy or sell 1000 shares. For example, if you think a company's share price is likely to rise fast over the coming months, you might buy a call option. A Megacorp June 650p call option costing 45p would cost you 1000 x 45p = £450. Come June, Megacorp's price hopefully will have risen to 700p. So you would exercise your contract, buy the shares at £650p and sell them immediately at 700p, making a £500 profit. Deduct the original contract premium for an overall profit of £50.

All this might seem a lot of effort for a profit of £50, especially when our example has ignored dealing costs and bid-offer spreads. So it is essential that you know what you're doing before you invest in derivatives.

ONLINE RESOURCES

As mentioned above, LIFFE (www.liffe.com) is the best place to start for derivatives price information and graphs of the underlying securities and indices. It has developed a section devoted to private investors. In the US the main derivatives exchange is the Chicago Board Options Exchange (www.cboe.com), which is also useful to find out all about this subject.

If you want to trade futures and options it is important to keep a close eye on the real price of the underlying security, so make sure you make full use of the sites recommended in Chapter 6.

The following sites are also useful:

INO Global (US)	www.ino.com
Futures Online (US)	www.futuresmag.com
FutureSource (US)	www.futuresource.com
Options Direct (UK)	www.options-direct.co.uk
Reuters Financial Futures	www.commods.reuters.com
Applied Derivatives	www.adtrading.com
Futures and OTC	www.fow.com

BROKERS

There aren't many online brokers offering futures and options trading, but Charles Schwab Europe was one of the first to offer options trading at least. The problem is that most online investors in the UK are still getting to grips with equities and funds, let alone derivatives. The take-up of options-dealing services hasn't been spectacular to say the least. Consequently there are only a few around.

Charles Schwab Europe	www.schwab-europe.com
Options Direct	www.options-direct.co.uk
Berkeley Futures	www.bfl.co.uk
GNI	www.gni.co.uk
IfX	www.ifx.co.uk
Sucden	www.sucden.co.uk

OPTIONS SOFTWARE

The internet is amazing in the sheer volume of free software and educational material that is available if you know where to look.

Below we list a couple of software sites that provide free programs to help you analyse options:

Optimum	www.warp9.org/nwsoft/index.html
Option Driver	www.download.com/optdrv32.zip

Bonds and gilts

A bond is like an IOU. You effectively loan money to a company or government in return for a fixed level of income (coupon) and the guaranteed return of your investment at the end of the bond's life (known as 'the maturity date'). There are lots of different types of bond, some maturing in a few years, some after twenty-five years. One advantage of bonds over shares is that bondholders are ahead of shareholders in the pecking order if the underlying company goes bust.

Very few people actually hold bonds until maturity and there is a global multi-billion dollar market in bonds. Although the maturity price – redemption price – and income level are fixed, the market prices of bonds can rise and fall just like shares. Prices are greatly affected by interest rates and inflation forecasts. If inflation is likely to take off, your fixed income will be worth much less as time goes by, so you'd expect to pay less for your bonds in the open market to compensate for this.

Bear in mind that a bond advertising a higher-than-average interest rate may indicate that the issuing company is actually quite risky. Safer companies feel they don't have to offer such high rates. And overall, the long-term return on bonds is lower than that achieved by shares. But bonds are useful for boosting income in retirement. A bond fund buys and sells a whole range of bonds in an attempt to achieve a fairly stable level of income for its investors. If the fund is within a Personal Equity Plan or Individual Savings Account, the income will be tax free too.

ONLINE RESOURCES

Despite the attraction of bonds in a well-balanced portfolio online resources are scarce.

Bonds Online (US)	www.bonds-online.com
Ample Interactive	
Investor	www.iii.co.uk/bonds
Bloomberg	www.bloomberg.co.uk
Kauders Portfolio	
Management	www.gilt.co.uk
Yahoo! Finance	http://uk.biz.yahoo.com/i/gilts.html

BROKERS

Looking for brokers that allow online purchasing of bonds and gilts is a frustrating task. It's as if nobody's heard of this sensible alternative to equities. I found only one, although there may be more by the time this book is published. Let's hope so.

DLJ Direct (www.dljdirect.co.uk) – account holders can invest in over 200 investment-grade bonds, including all UK Government bonds (gilts), bonds issued by the European Investment Bank (EIB) and Blue Chip corporate bonds.

You can also buy government bonds (gilts) over the Post Office counter through the National Savings Stock Register (NSSR).

Pensions

Pensions have hardly featured online so far because they are generally considered to be too complicated for most people to buy on an 'execution-only' – no advice – basis. Most people need advice when it comes to retirement planning, so pensions have traditionally been sold by independent financial advisers. But things are changing. The personal pension mis-selling scandal dented confidence in the market to such an extent that the Government devised a new, simpler and cheaper product – the stakeholder pension.

It was launched in April 2001 and aimed at average and below-average earners who have yet to make any private provision for retirement. You can invest a maximum of £3600 and annual management charges are limited to 1 per cent. Many pension providers had already tailored their products to meet the Government's charges-access-terms (CAT) standards before April 2001.

The simplicity of the product and its low cost makes it ideal to sell online. Indeed, many industry experts believe that the internet is the only way pension providers will be able to market these pensions cost effectively given the cap on charges.

There are a number of useful personal finance websites to visit if you want to find out more about stakeholder pensions and how much you need to contribute to reach a certain level of income in retirement. My favourites are:

This Is Money	www.thisismoney.com
Ample Interactive Investor	www.ample.com
FT Your Money	www.ftyourmoney.com

When researching pension options online, it is a good idea to find out how much your state pension might be worth at retirement age (currently sixty-five for men and sixty for women). You can fill in an application form (BR19) on the Department for Work and Pensions website (www.dss.gov.uk) (formerly the DSS). If that doesn't spur you into increasing your personal pension contributions, nothing will. There are plenty of guides, leaflets and links to other government departments on the site.

Incidentally, if you feel you may have been a victim of the mis-selling scandal, check out the Financial Services Authority (FSA) website (www.fsa.gov.uk). It tells you how to find out if you have cause for complaint and what to do about it.

STAKEHOLDER PENSIONS ONLINE

No one is ever going to make pensions sexy, but even the most hedonistic twenty-something is starting to realise that they are a necessary evil. At least the internet is helping to make the process of starting one relatively painless and the new stakeholder pension is a good place to start.

To help you decide whether a stakeholder pension is right for you, the FSA has produced some helpful decision trees. You can use the interactive online version or download it in PDF format for completion offline. (You need a free program called Adobe Acrobat Reader to read PDF files. If you don't have it, the FSA provides a link to the Adobe website.)

After wading through a wordy twelve-page introductory guide, you eventually get to the decision tree. There are also useful tables giving indications of how much you would need to save each month in a stakeholder pension to achieve various retirement income levels. Sobering stuff.

The stakeholder legislation allowed pension providers to accept online applications without the need for a written signature. So now you can apply online, set up regular payments and make a lump sum contribution using your debit card. All you need to hand are your bank details and National Insurance number.

Below are some of best online stakeholder pension providers:

Discount Pensions (www.discountpensions.co.uk) – Discount Pensions is a pensions broker, offering products from seven providers so far – AXA Sun Life, CGU Life, Clerical Medical, Norwich Union, Scottish Equitable, Scottish Widows and Standard

Life. The model is much the same as the investment fund super-markets – lower charges and commissions than you would normally pay if you went through a financial adviser. Discount Pensions offers no advice and commission is 1 per cent with a £25 handling fee on top. The introduction of the stakeholder pensions means that IFAs will be put under more pressure to reimburse some or all of the commission they receive from pension providers. So be on the lookout for plenty of discount deals on IFA websites over the next couple of years.

Virgin Direct (www.virgindirect.co.uk) – Virgin Direct's pension website is brilliant in its simplicity and clarity. For once, Flash animation is used to liven up the site without slowing things down and obscuring the main message. All the relevant information is clearly and logically displayed, and does not overwhelm pension novices. Virgin's pension is based on its FTSE All-Share index-tracking fund, which is meant to track the performance of the stock market as a whole.

Virgin is quick to point out that over the long-term – twenty years, say – the percentage of fund managers outperforming the stock market falls to zero, making tracker funds ideal investments for low-cost pensions. As you reach ten years before retirement, your fund is gradually shifted into lower-risk investments, such as gilts and cash funds. You can apply and invest online, but there is also telephone support from fully qualified advisers should you want it.

Legal & General (www.landg.co.uk) – L&G offers some twenty stakeholder-compliant funds. Each fund's performance statistics are readily available on the site. If you don't want the hassle of choosing for yourself, the basic option is L&G's index tracker fund. The online application process takes around twenty to thirty minutes and if you need help at any time you can have a live text conversation with an adviser or simply ring up. The L&G website isn't as pretty or simple as Virgin's, but it is still very good, and L&G's tracker funds have a better performance record.

Charcolonline (www.charcolonline.co.uk) – Charcolonline, the online financial services broker owned by Bradford & Bingley,

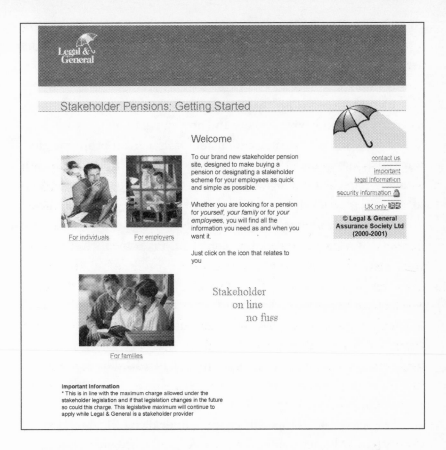

provides a very thorough online guide and pension selection tool. You answer questions aimed at assessing your investment priorities and narrowing down the choice of providers. Eventually you are given a shortlist of providers ranked according to how closely they meet your priorities. You can then select two from the list and compare their charges, fund choice and performance. If you like what you see you can apply online there and then. Charcolonline's selection tool is very sophisticated and the sheer amount of information can be a little overwhelming, but proposed site redesigns should solve this problem.

SELF-INVESTED PERSONAL PENSIONS (SIPPS)

The demise of Equitable Life, the life insurance company that promised more than it could deliver, has left many people uneasy about the apparent lack of control they have over their own retirement funds. So a growing number of do-it-yourself investors are seizing control and making their own investment decisions through SIPPs.

Launched in 1988, SIPPs are flexible schemes that allow investors to choose when, where and how much to invest (within the Inland Revenue limits). You can include commercial property, gilts, warrants, shares and funds in your pension portfolio, while still enjoying the usual tax benefits of a personal pension. This freedom to mix and match helps to spread the risk of one of your investments or fund managers performing badly. Also, when stock markets are particularly volatile, you can convert your investments to cash and wait until the situation improves.

To date, SIPPs have remained the preserve of rich investors thanks to hefty set-up and administration charges. You could expect to pay a set-up fee of at least £500 and more in annual management charges with a traditional SIPP. And with dealing charges on top, they were only suitable for those with at least £50,000 to £100,000 to invest. But now the internet is helping to reduce costs dramatically, opening up SIPPs to a much wider audience.

For example, Sippdeal (www.sippdeal.co.uk), founded in October 2000 by actuarial consultant A. J. Bell, provides online and telephone dealing in a wide range of investments for a set-up charge of just £100. Amazingly, there's no annual management fee. Dealing charges are £15 to £30 for shares, gilts and warrants, and a chunky 1 per cent of the amount invested for funds, up to a maximum of £100. Sippdeal claims basic-rate tax relief from the Revenue on your behalf, with higher-rate taxpayers claiming the extra through their tax returns.

The site is rudimentary and lacks research resources, but as commercial director Fergus Lyons points out: 'It gets the job done at a very competitive price.' Lyons says the site is about to be revamped and new products, such as SIPPs for children, have been launched recently. International dealing in US and European stocks is also expected early in 2002. Sippdeal offers excellent value for money.

If you want to keep your investments under one roof, a fully-fledged online stockbroker may be a better bet. Some investors prefer immediate access to research tools and to have all their PEPs, ISAs, shares and pensions on the same site. Of course, you pay for this kind of convenience.

Sippdeal administers the SIPPs offered by brokers Charles Schwab (www.schwab-europe.com) and Killik & Co. (www.killik.co.uk). But don't expect the same charging structure. Schwab's set-up fee is £135, plus there's a quarterly administration fee of 0.125 per cent on the first £100,000 of the fund's value. This translates as a flat £500 annual fee on funds worth £100,000 or more. Schwab is good for functionality, but heavy on the pocket. Killik is more reasonable, mirroring the Sippdeal charging structure, but if you plan to deal often you'll be stung by the broker's £40 minimum dealing charge.

DLJ Direct (www.dljdirect.co.uk) uses Personal Pension Management Limited, the UK's largest SIPP administrator, instead of Sippdeal. With a £200 set-up fee and a quarterly administration charge of 0.15 per cent of the fund's value (£600 annually on funds worth £100,000 or more), DLJ is pretty pricey. But the site is attractive and replete with useful research tools for the self-motivated investor.

Nothing Ventured (www.nothing-ventured.com), the online broker owned by Durlacher, offers a whole host of resources for the serious investor. But you pay for this level of service. The set-up fee is £150 and a 0.75 per cent annual administration fee on the first £100,000 of the fund's value means a flat £750 a year for funds worth more than £100,000. Despite these charges, an online SIPP is still far cheaper than the traditional version and gives investors far more control over their own investments.

Spread-betting and contracts for difference

If you don't get a big enough adrenalin rush from taking speculative punts on dot.com start-ups you could always try some racier forms of investment. I've lumped these types of investment together mainly because there is a small group of online brokers that seem to specialise in them.

As this book is primarily aimed at novice and intermediate investors who may be getting to grips with the internet for the first time, I don't want to devote too much space to forms of investment that are highly risky and more akin to casino games than long-term investing. More experienced investors can make use of the websites recommended below.

SPREAD-BETTING

This extreme form of investing was dreamed up by thrill-seeking City boys looking to spice up their lives. Basically, spread-betting allows you to bet on anything you like with the profits or losses related to how closely you predict the outcome of a particular variable result, such as the number of goals scored in a match, or the number of points a market index falls by over a set period.

The closer you are to the right answer, the greater your winnings and vice versa. It is very, very risky and only suited to aggressive investors, rich enough or desperate enough to gamble big time. Yes, you can make a lot of money, but you can also lose spectacularly in a frighteningly short space of time.

Despite the risks, private investors have been drawn increasingly to spread-betting as an alternative to a stock market currently at levels it reached four years ago. With investments going backwards and some investors sitting on massive losses, any hope of rapid recovery is tempting for some. But don't say I didn't warn you!

CONTRACTS FOR DIFFERENCE (CFDS)

CFDs are gradually gaining acceptance as a cheaper way to deal in equities. With CFDs you don't actually buy the underlying shares, just the price of them, so there are no dealing charges. You also buy on margin, as is common in the US. This means you only stump up a proportion of the deal size – typically 20 per cent. This kind of leveraging can magnify your gains, but also your losses, so it's not for the faint-hearted.

BROKERS

Berkeley Futures	www.bfl.co.uk
Cantor Index	www.cantorindex.com
City Index	www.cityindex.co.uk
Deal4Free	www.deal4free.com
Financial Spreads	www.finspreads.com
GNI	www.gni.co.uk
IG Index	www.indexdirect.co.uk
IG Markets	www.igshares.com
SpreadEx	http://212.47.84.178/

8
Personal Finance

Introduction

Financial services and the internet were made for each other. Most money is digital these days, just numbers transferring from one computer to another. We use credit and debit cards, make regular payments by standing order and direct debit, pay bills and transfer money between accounts online. The prevalence of paper-based systems, such as cash and chequebooks, is gradually dwindling.

Laws are being changed to give legal status to digital signatures so that we can open accounts, apply for loans and other financial products online without resorting to annoying paper forms, written signatures and a reliance on 'snail mail'. Those who are embracing this technological revolution are gaining freedom – no more bank queues and wasted lunch hours – and a far greater control over their finances. Owing to the '24–7' nature of the internet, we can keep on top of things more efficiently than ever before.

What's more, the internet is so good at sifting and sorting vast quantities of data that comparing products – even complicated beasts like mortgages – has become easy. This 'transparency', as it is called, has had a wonderful effect on competition. On the web there is nowhere for uncompetitive products and providers to hide. Their flaws are exposed for the whole world to see. Product providers have little choice but to respond, or, eventually, go out of business altogether.

In this respect the internet has proved an empowering tool for the consumer, saving us time and money. In this chapter we show you how to use the web to find the best deals on a range of other financial products. After all, the more money you save on these, the more you will have left over for investing.

General personal finance websites

There are several very useful personal finance websites that make it their job to help you shop around for the best products and educate you about all things financial. They should be your first port of call when shopping around. These are my favourites:

This Is Money	www.thisismoney.com
MX Moneyextra	www.moneyextra.com
Ample Interactive Investor	www.ample.com
Moneynet	www.moneynet.co.uk

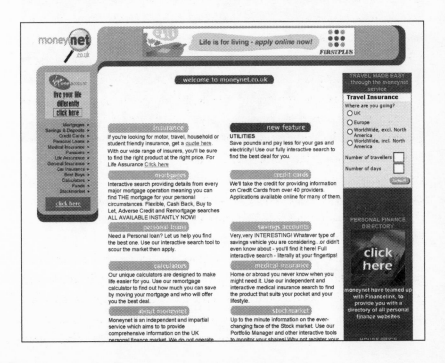

Moneysupermarket	www.moneysupermarket.com
FT Your Money	www.ftyourmoney.com
Moneyfacts	www.moneyfacts.co.uk
CreditWeb	www.creditweb.co.uk
FIND (financial website directory)	www.find.co.uk

| Moneywise Magazine | www.moneywise.co.uk |
| Charcolonline | www.charcolonline.co.uk |

Current accounts

Banking on the internet is growing rapidly in popularity as people warm to the convenience and greater financial control it gives them. Around 7 million people now bank online according to the British

Bankers Association. Why waste time queuing when you can access your accounts, transfer funds and pay bills from the comfort of your own home and office at a time that suits you? The advantages clearly outweigh any lingering concerns about security. But with nearly sixty providers offering some form of online banking facility, how do you choose the best?

A lot depends on whether you're simply after the highest rate of interest on your cash or full current account functionality. Some banks have happily managed to combine both. Another consideration is whether you're happy dealing with an internet-only bank or prefer to have access to a branch network. In reality, the only real drawback of an internet bank is having to deposit cheques by post rather than at the branch. And with the likes of Intelligent Finance, Smile and Cahoot offering rates of interest that put the high-street banks to shame, such disadvantages seem trivial.

In this section I recommend five banks that offer traditional current account features, such as chequebook, debit card and overdraft facility, as well as the ability to view balances, transfer funds and pay bills online. All the accounts featured offered free banking while in credit and most offered telephone banking as well.

Smile (www.smile.co.uk) – owned by the Co-operative Bank, is a wonderfully simple and accessible design coupled with an excellent range of services and good customer service. Its gross interest rate on credit balances is one of the best around. I've only heard positive comments about Smile and it is also the only bank to receive accreditation from the British Standards Institution for its security. The lack of a telephone banking facility is the only real drawback.

Cahoot (www.cahoot.com) – the Abbey National's standalone net bank, often has the highest interest rates on the market. It offers crisp website design and technological innovation, such as mobile banking via free WAP-enabled mobile phone and the ability to set up standing orders online. The only doubt surrounds its reliability. Cahoot famously crashed on the day it launched and anecdotal evidence suggests there are still some gremlins in the works, such as occasional log-in failures. Let's hope they sort these out eventually.

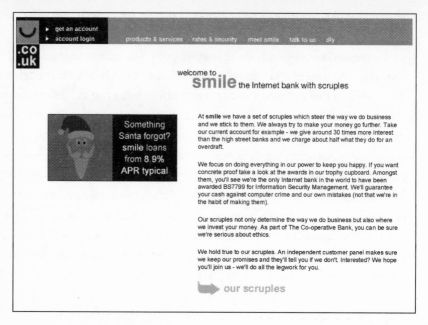

Intelligent Finance (www.if.com) – from the Halifax, pools your current and savings account balances to give you higher rates of interest and help reduce the interest paid on borrowings as well. It's the kind of all-in-one banking offered by the likes of Virgin and the Woolwich. Even if you don't need all that, the vanilla current account is competitive, plus there's mobile banking and traditional telephone banking support.

Nationwide (www.nationwide.co.uk) – a traditional building society with a branch network for those who like a 'belt-and-braces' approach to their banking. One of the pioneers of online banking, Nationwide offers truly excellent functionality, including the ability to order duplicate statements and view credit card statements online. It was the first to offer mobile banking, too. It doesn't often come top in the interest rate tables (I suspect because it has that large branch network to pay for) but it is a good all-round performer.

First Direct (www.firstdirect.com) – has also won critical acclaim. It offers a solid range of services backed by its tried and tested telephone banking operation. The fact that it is owned by HSBC also means that you do have access to a branch network. Rather miserly credit balance interest rates let it down, though.

The main reason we don't switch to more competitive accounts is the hassle involved, especially with all those direct debits and standing orders to take care of. The new online banks are all too aware of this. Intelligent Finance has a dedicated team to help you transfer your account and Smile also helps with pre-written letters on its site that you can print off and sign. And in a recent report, the Treasury proposes fining banks if they fail to hand over the customer's list of direct debits and standing orders to the new bank within five days. The whole account-switching process should not take longer than five weeks, the report says. The days of the old-fashioned, high-charging banks are numbered.

Savings accounts

It was a tough time for savers in 2001. The Bank of England repeatedly chipped away at base interest rates so that they finished at 4 per cent after starting the year at around 6 per cent. In many cases income from savings was slashed by a third – worrying for people who need extra income to supplement pensions. Although many economists believe we may have reached the bottom of the interest rate cycle, the threat of global recession could mean that we stay at this level for some time, especially given that UK inflation seems well under control. All this means that savers have to work extra hard to find a good deal.

The internet-only banks do not have large branch networks to maintain, so they can pass on these savings to customers in the form of higher interest rates. With greater reliance on automation and eschewing paper-based processes wherever possible, they can also keep administration costs to a minimum. This is the theory anyway.

Using the excellent Moneyfacts personal finance site to find out the latest savings rates, it seems that Abbey National's (www.abbeynational.co.uk) e-Saver internet-only account is still top of the table (in December 2001), paying 4.9 per cent gross (including an introductory bonus). The minimum investment is £500. You can apply online but, ironically for an internet account, new customers still have to send in utility bills or credit card statements to prove their address. They also have to make the initial payment by cheque. I find this baffling.

You wouldn't know it from the behaviour of the UK banking industry, but digital signatures are now legal. If you had your own digital certificate you could prove who you are at the click of a mouse. It would speed up application processes enormously. You can open a share-dealing account online in minutes and fund it using a debit card. You can do the same with stakeholder pensions and Individual Savings Accounts (ISAs). So why not savings accounts? Banks mutter about money laundering regulations, but digital certificates would easily take care of those and the money banks saved on administration could be ploughed back into higher interest rates for savers.

Another good internet savings account comes from Northern Rock (www.northernrock.co.uk), paying 4.75 per cent gross on its Tracker Online account. The minimum investment is only £1. You can apply online via the Moneyfacts site. Northern Rock's secure online application system is admirable, going as far as issuing your security code and account number within five minutes. After that you receive a welcome letter with information on how you can fund the account. Abbey National take note: electronic bank-to-bank transfers are allowed.

The main drawback with these internet-only saver accounts is that they tend to pay interest yearly. So if you need to make a withdrawal before then, you get no interest on that money. As a general rule, the longer you can tie up your savings the better the interest rate you'll get. For example, Manchester Building Society (www.themanchester.co.uk) was paying 4.85 per cent on its ninety-day notice account. Again, interest is paid yearly. But with interest rates likely to rise rather than fall over the next year or so it probably isn't a good idea to go for fixed-rate products, unless you prize certainty above all else.

If you want or need monthly income from your savings you

usually have to accept a slightly lower rate of interest. Both Abbey National and Northern Rock offer monthly interest versions of their internet savings accounts that were paying 4.79 per cent and 4.5 per cent gross respectively. And Cahoot (www.cahoot.com), Abbey National's internet-only bank, was offering 4.36 per cent on its monthly-interest-paying current account. How long it can sustain this rate remains to be seen, but it certainly offers value for money at the moment.

Savers sometimes forget that they can protect £3000 of their savings from tax in a cash ISA every year. Smile (www.smile.co.uk), Co-operative Bank's superb internet-only bank, was paying 4.75 per cent gross on its cash ISA. Interest is paid yearly, so be sure you won't need to make withdrawals. You can apply securely online quoting your National Insurance number, bank account and employment details. The account is usually set up and running within a few days. Northern Rock – the current king of the savings heap – trumped Smile with a cash ISA rate of 4.8 per cent.

Mortgages

With interest rates at their lowest since the Sixties, it is a wonderful time to remortgage. But with nearly 5000 mortgage products on the market, shopping around for the best-value loan can still be a daunting task. Fortunately, one of the internet's main strengths is sifting and sorting vast quantities of data, making shopping around much easier.

One of the best financial sites for mortgages is Moneynet (www.moneynet.co.uk). It scours several thousand mortgages from over 100 lenders. Its remortgage calculator is excellent because it works out the savings you could make by switching lender, including any redemption penalties and arrangement fees you would have to pay. All you do is fill in the boxes, giving details of your current mortgage, such as the interest rate, size of loan and redemption penalty (if any), then choose the types of mortgage you are interested in. You can restrict the search to one type of mortgage – such as fixed-rate – if you like, or select the whole range, from standard variable to cashback. You can also choose to exclude loans that have redemption penalties applicable beyond any discounted, capped or fixed-rate period.

Moneynet assumes you'll have to pay £400 in legal costs and £200 to have your home valued. It includes these figures when working out the savings. What's more, you can select the time period for the calculation to coincide with the number of years you think you might keep the loan. This is especially important because low initial interest rates on discounted mortgages can give a misleading impression. Once the discounted period is over your payments may rise sharply but redemption penalties may trap you in the loan. So choosing a five-year period, say, for the comparison will take this effect into account and give you a truer picture of the total costs involved.

Once you've selected all the parameters for the search, simply click on 'submit' and up pops a detailed table showing the best deals that Moneynet has found plus the savings you'd make over your chosen time period. You can click on a link to see details of the loans, including the monthly repayments, and you can also apply online. The application process is handled by an affiliated firm of independent financial advisers called Inter-Alliance. Its representatives are available, too, to give mortgage advice over the phone.

As a safety precaution, check that the mortgage particulars are correct with the lender. I have come across instances where the databases have been misleading, putting some products at the top of the table unjustly. This doesn't happen often, but it is something to be wary of.

One problem with mortgage comparison sites is that you can't be sure they're covering the entire market. Not all lenders co-operate with them. And specialist mortgage brokers are often able to negotiate exclusive deals that won't be listed on such sites. So it makes sense to check out some of the brokers as well. One of the best is Charcolonline (www.charcolonline.co.uk). It provides access to around 500 loans from forty-five lenders, several of which are exclusive to it. If you apply online you don't pay any broker fees and advice is available by phone.

The site lists Charcolonline's selection of 'best buys' for

different types of mortgage, including specialist categories, such as divorcees or budding landlords. You can use the site's 'Mortgage Wizard' – a detailed Q&A – that eventually recommends specific loans to suit your needs. Although Charcolonline is one of the best brokers around, I have found its site rather clunky and prone to crashes on several occasions. If you can put up with such minor frustrations you should still end up with a good deal.

Another impressive broker is CreditWeb (www.creditweb.co.uk). It claims to scan 4500 mortgages daily for the best deals. Using the website is tricky, though. You have to

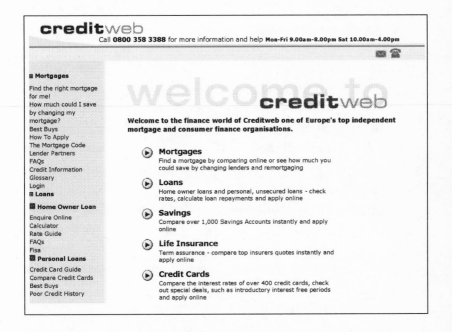

complete an exhaustive online Q&A, giving details of your income and the type of mortgage you're after, for example. Then you're shown the details of the recommended mortgages, but not the names of the lenders. To receive a full quotation you have to fill in another form before the lender's details are revealed. And when I tested the search engine I specifically opted for loans that had no early redemption penalties, but the 'best buy' list still included them. The filtering system hadn't worked. CreditWeb was redeemed by the quality of the telephone support. I received helpful and impartial advice.

Personal loans

The market for online loans is very dynamic because they are such simple products. The credit-checking procedure doesn't have to be so rigorous because the amounts loaned are usually not more than £15,000. It's also easy for people to work out monthly payments using online calculators. And as more and more lenders are offering online applications, we're in for a sustained period of intense competition and lower borrowing rates.

The web helps lenders to market their products more effectively and economically, but it also leaves them more exposed to competition. With the addition of helpful calculators on websites, potential borrowers can spot an uncompetitive rate a mile off these days. This transparency is helping to bring annual percentage rates (APRs) down to well below 10 per cent and has provided opportunities for niche loan providers to steal customers from under the noses of the big banks.

As most lenders are beginning to offer online application forms for loans, there's no room to list them all. Just look at the personal-loans section of FIND (www.find.co.uk), the online financial services directory. In the meantime, here's a quick step-by-step guide to finding a cheap online loan.

First, compare rates. Try a few of the general personal-finance websites mentioned at the start of this chapter and use their search facilities to find you some 'best buys'. These sites also contain a lot of useful guide notes and articles pointing out the features to watch for when taking out a loan. It's important to use several 'infomediary' sites, as some lenders don't supply information to particular sites and some sites are not as comprehensive as others or as conscientious about keeping the information up to date.

When reviewing the tables make sure you know whether the

figures include payment protection insurance or not. If you like what you see, you can just click on the link through to the lender, if such a link has been set up. Otherwise you can open a new browser window and go direct to the lender's website. Again, use FIND if you don't know the address. It's that simple, which is why the online personal-loans sector is going to become one of the most dynamic in online financial services.

The Royal Bank of Scotland (www.rbs.co.uk) is one of the most innovative of the banks when it comes to online services. It is offering almost instant online 'approval in principle' for its personal loans. Once again, it is leading the way for others to follow. Smile, the internet bank owned by the Co-operative Bank, offers online approval too, plus the ability to view your loan and manage your loan repayments from within your online bank account.

There are also competitive rates being offered by car websites, since car finance is the most popular use of the personal loan. For example, Autobytel (www.autobytel.co.uk), in conjunction with its loan provider Alliance & Leicester, was offering loans from around 7.9 per cent APR.

Credit cards

We simply can't get enough of plastic. There are over 100 million credit, debit and charge cards in the UK, representing 169 cards for every 100 people, according to Datamonitor, the research group. And now that the market is more competitive than ever, low introductory rates are encouraging borrowers to switch card issuers at the drop of a hat in pursuit of lower borrowing costs. Customer loyalty is at an all-time low.

Around 70 per cent of credit card holders do not pay off their borrowings each month. The Bank of England says we owed a staggering £34 billion on our credit cards at the end of 2000. So shopping around for the lowest credit card APR is critical if you want to save potentially hundreds of pounds a year.

Using a financial comparison website such as MX Moneyextra (www.moneyextra.com) is a good place to start. It compares rates on hundreds of different cards. Simply estimate your monthly debit balance and select your current credit card from the list provided. MX Moneyextra's calculator will then work out how much you could save over a time period of your choice. If your average monthly balance was around £1500 on one of the dearest cards, you could save around £400 over two years by switching to the cheapest.

MX Moneyextra's calculator also allows you to narrow your search in a number of ways. For instance, you can exclude cards that charge an annual fee or which don't offer an interest-free period. The ability to select the time period over which you want the comparisons to be made is very useful. Some low introductory rates last for only a few months, so working out the savings over a longer period takes the issuer's higher rate into account. This gives a truer picture of the potential savings. The fact that you can apply online in the majority of cases wins MX Moneyextra extra Brownie points in my book.

It's a good idea to try more than one financial comparison site in case product details aren't up to date or certain card issuers do not co-operate with the first site you try. Another site worth trying is Moneysupermarket. It compares details on over 300 cards, giving you the option to choose the right card for you whether you're a borrower or someone who religiously pays off the bill each month. It performs most of the same functions as the MX Moneyextra site.

Moneyfacts offers a pleasant no-nonsense approach, simply making 'best buy' selections based on different standard criteria. For example, you can see which standard credit cards offer the best introductory rates on balance transfers or select Platinum and Gold cards only. If you just borrow occasionally and don't have a big debit balance to transfer, you'll want a card with a low APR on purchases, an interest-free period and no annual fee. Moneyfacts gives you such a list without fuss. Once it persuades more of the card issuers to accept online applications via the site, the service will be even better.

If you never borrow but still want to get the most out of your credit card, cashback and loyalty points schemes could entice you to switch. Egg (www.egg.com), the internet bank, offers its credit card customers 0.5 per cent cashback on all purchases made with the card. You can apply and manage your account entirely online, including transferring balances from other cards to your Egg card. My only reservation is about the reliability of the Egg system. It has been notoriously prone to gremlins in the past, but Egg says it has ironed out most of these by now.

For a list of the major credit card issuers that also offer loyalty schemes, choose this option when using Moneyextra's comparison calculator.

Life insurance

You don't necessarily need independent financial advice to buy term life assurance. It's a simple product that lasts for a specific number of years and pays out a fixed sum on death within that period. All you need to work out is how much death benefit you need to protect your loved ones if you pop your clogs prematurely.

Many of us put off buying insurance because we don't like thinking about death. But if you have dependents and you don't want them to suffer financially it's a must. Using the net can speed up the process of buying cover at the cheapest price, so there are really very few excuses left for not biting the bullet.

I shopped around for a joint life twenty-year term policy that would pay out £250,000 on the death of either partner (both aged thirty-four). I started with a few of the many online life insurance brokers, choosing at random from financial directories FIND (www.find.co.uk) and e-Insurance Directory (www.e-insurancedirectory.com).

Bolton-based Online Life Insurance (www.onlinelifeinsurance.co.uk) collates quotes from thirteen insurers and e-mails you the best one. The site is simple and clear. Just fill in the online form saying what type and level of cover you want, and submit the request. The only trouble is it takes twelve hours before you receive your e-mail quotation. Eventually I was quoted £30.25 a month courtesy of the Norwich Union and Online

Life Insurance. It automatically sent me some application forms by post.

Ironically, you can sometimes receive a better offer from another broker for exactly the same policy underwritten by the same insurer. This is because intermediaries can rebate some or all of the commission they receive from the insurance company and give it to customers in the form of lower premiums. Investment Discounts Online (www.theidol.com) does just this and quoted me £24. A lot of people don't realise that you can use your internet findings as ammunition, haggling with intermediaries to rebate more of their commission and so bring down the premium.

Idol's site is neatly designed and the quotation process is straightforward. Just give details such as your date of birth, occupation and type of cover required, then submit your request. Idol consults a panel of nineteen insurers for the best quote. Again, the quote took twelve hours to arrive and I couldn't apply online, but Idol still deserves a recommendation.

Direct Life and Pension Services (www.dlps.co.uk) scored a hit with a simple, fast site that gave me instant online quotations from the best three major insurers from ten on its panel. Although they weren't as competitive as Idol, they were close. The site could be improved with the addition of an online application facility.

It is always a good idea to try some direct insurers for comparison. Direct Line (www.directline.com) boasts about the speed of its quotation systems but it seldom comes top of the tables and couldn't beat the quotes I received elsewhere. Legal & General (www.landg.com) came up with a reasonably competitive quote of £30.49 that included free terminal illness cover, plus you could apply online. L&G seems to be one of the few big insurance companies to have got to grips with the web and fully understood its potential as a powerful marketing and administrative tool.

Looking for cheap life insurance on the web entails a lot of repetitive form filling, so make sure you have activated the 'auto complete' option in your web browser. This function recognises words and numbers that you've written before, and automatically completes application form boxes when you type in the first letter or number required. In Microsoft Internet Explorer, click on 'Tools', 'Internet Options', 'Content' then 'AutoComplete' and check the relevant boxes.

Car insurance

When our motor insurance policy comes up for renewal each year the premium never seems to go down, no matter how many years' no-claims discount we have built up. It's the first law of motor insurance. Shopping around is an absolute must – it can save us hundreds of pounds. With over 2000 insurance brokers and agents, and eighty insurers in the market, the internet is becoming an essential assistant in the quest for lower premiums.

The net offers several advantages over the telephone. First, it never closes, so you can get a quote whenever you like. Second, it's much better at handling large amounts of information. After filling in a lengthy online quotation form you can usually save it and come back to it later using a unique 'session number' or password. This is useful because it allows you to play around with the variables – such as the voluntary excess you are prepared to pay – and see what effect it has on the premium being offered.

Third, insurance 'supermarkets' are making it easier for us to compare policies and receive the most competitive quote from a panel of insurers. This saves time and hassle. Ringing round several direct insurers and brokers answering the same questions over and over again is a chore most of us would happily avoid. Last, direct insurers are increasingly offering discounts to motorists if they buy their insurance online. It is cheaper for insurance companies to sell insurance over the web than over the phone.

For example, the AA (www.theaa.com) one of the largest insurance brokers, offers a 5 per cent discount for online purchases. To get a quick quote from its panel of sixteen insurers you spend just five minutes filling in the application form. The service is quick and easy to use because the AA makes several assumptions about the type of cover you're looking for and the type of driver you are.

You can change these assumptions and alter the premium if you need to before buying online. Once you've taken out a policy you can also change your details and make renewals online. The AA now derives 40 per cent of its quotes from the web and has sold more than 80,000 policies online since 1999. It must be doing something right.

Egg (www.egg.com), the online financial services company, also offers an insurance supermarket. It has a bright and friendly design with a quote promised after just six questions. If you like the indicative quote you can then click through for a more detailed version and buy online. High marks for simplicity and ease of use. Other supermarkets worth checking out included Moneynet (www.moneynet.co.uk), Autobytel (www.autobytel.co.uk) and Insure (www.insure.co.uk). They are all admirably straightforward to use.

Despite the demise of Screentrade, one of the earliest online insurance brokers, we're beginning to see a lot more insurance supermarkets around. This is because websites can buy 'off-the-shelf' quotation engines from the likes of Xelector and Cox Insurance. For example, Egg's engine is supplied by Cox, Autobytel uses Xelector. The only problem with this is that you're likely to end up with similar quotes from different websites if they use the same quotation engine. You could end up wasting time in the belief that you're shopping around when you're not.

But don't assume that an insurance supermarket will always find you the best premium. It won't. There are just so many variables in motor insurance – your age, address, car type and claims history – that it is impossible to say where the cheapest quotes will be found. In the end you still have to try several channels, including the traditional high-street and telephone brokers.

Also, go to some of the big, direct insurers directly. Morethan (www.morethan.com), the new online service from the UK's largest motor insurer, Royal & Sun Alliance, is worthwhile visiting for comparison purposes. But be warned: on a few occasions that I have visited the site it has proved a little cranky, sometimes refusing to give me a quote at all. All new sites tend to have their share of gremlins, but you would have thought that a company the size of

Royal & Sun Alliance might have spent more time perfecting the service before launching it.

Direct Line (www.directline.com) has made great strides in simplifying the online quotation process. The TV advert claims you can get a quote in two minutes. You can when everything's working properly. At least you can save your quote and return to it later using a password system. But however attractive the website, when it comes to car insurance price is the bottom line. Direct Line doesn't often feature in 'best buy' tables.

Eagle Star Direct (www.eaglestardirect.co.uk) is pretty competitive and Admiral (www.admiral-insurance.co.uk) has a good reputation. Its website is clear and straightforward to use. You get a provisional 'quick quote' after ten questions so you don't waste time. If it's in the right ball park you can go for the full quote. Buying online is easy – just pay by plastic over a secure server.

Home insurance

I dream of receiving a letter from my home insurer congratulating me on foiling the burglars, ducking acts of God, and staving off the depredations of clumsy kids and frolicksome pets. In celebration of my prudence and good fortune the insurer vastly reduces my renewal premium and begs me to stay loyal. But it never happens. The premium rises inexorably under some inflationary law devised and understood only by insurance actuaries. So it's on to the web to shop around for a better deal.

Before starting, gather a few details to help you fill in the online quotation forms. For example, you normally need to know the approximate year your property was built, its rebuilding cost and the replacement value of your home contents. This information is usually on the renewal premium sent by your existing insurer. But if you are taking out insurance for the first time, the Association of British Insurers (www.abi.org.uk) offers useful tables and calculators to help you work out rebuilding costs. It also provides lots of useful guides to the subject and is well worth a look to help you decide which type of cover you need and what steps you can take to help reduce your premiums.

If you haven't updated the contents 'sum assured' for several years, it may be worth going through your belongings again and redoing the calculation. It's surprising how many more possessions we can accumulate over the years.

When shopping around online for a better home insurance quote there are two main routes to take. One is to go through a broker who will scour tens, if not hundreds, of policies looking for the lowest quote based on your chosen criteria. The other is to go direct to insurer websites and use their quotation engines.

Using a few brokers and comparing their best rates with a few direct insurers is often a good idea. Ironically, you can sometimes get a better deal going through an online broker than from the insurer direct because the broker may be prepared to rebate commission it normally receives from insurance companies. Cheaper marketing and product distribution online makes this possible. You can find lists of broker and insurer websites by using financial directories, such as FIND and e-Insurance Directory (see above).

One impressive online broker is the Insurance Centre (www.theinsurancecentre.co.uk). It garners quotes from 450 policies and provides plenty of explanatory stuff about the ins and outs of home insurance. Just fill in the online questionnaire – it takes about five minutes – submit it, then up pops the best quote a few seconds later. You can alter the cover criteria, adding accidental-damage cover to buildings and contents, for example, to see what effect this has on the premium. If you like the quote, just ring up and apply.

The AA (www.theaa.com) is one of the better-known brokers thanks to its successful TV advertising campaign, but you shouldn't assume that this makes it the most competitive. It offers a 5 per cent discount on normal policy premiums if you apply online. The quotation engine is thorough, asking for precise details as to the security of French doors, for example. Once you've completed it you're supplied with the best quote it can find.

It is very important to look beyond the headline premium being quoted and find out exactly the extent of the cover. Home insurance policies can be fiendishly complex so you may not be making comparisons on a like-for-like basis. Also, quick quotations are possible because the insurer makes a number of assumptions about the cover you are after and the type of property you live in. Make sure that these assumptions are correct. If they're not, you may be in breach of the policy terms and conditions right from the start.

Other online brokers worth checking out include InsuranceWide (www.insurancewide.com) and Quoteline Direct (www.quotelinedirect.co.uk). For some comparisons with direct insurers try a random selection from the FIND directory.

Travel insurance

Around 35 million of us go on holiday each year and we should all have some sort of insurance in case things go wrong. Most of us buy policies from the travel agent at the same time as booking our holiday – convenient but expensive. The Consumers' Association says we can pay up to five times more than we need to this way. Using the web to compare prices is the best way to keep your holiday insurance costs down.

The web's price transparency is injecting some much-needed competition into the £400 million travel insurance market. Egg, the online bank, slashed its premiums by up to 25 per cent in 2001. And most of the big insurance companies, such as Eagle Star Direct (www.eaglestardirect.co.uk), Norwich Union Direct (www.norwichuniondirect.co.uk) and Churchill (www.churchill.com), now provide online quotations and discounts of up to 10 per cent for buying online.

As a general rule, avoid the high street banks and big brand travel agents like the plague. There are two chances of finding the cheapest policy from them – fat and slim. You're far better off going to specialists, such as Direct Travel Insurance (www.direct-travel.co.uk) and World Travel Direct (www.worldtraveldirect.com). There are also dozens of online insurance brokers and personal finance supermarkets that search a large panel of insurers for the best price and the right type of cover for you.

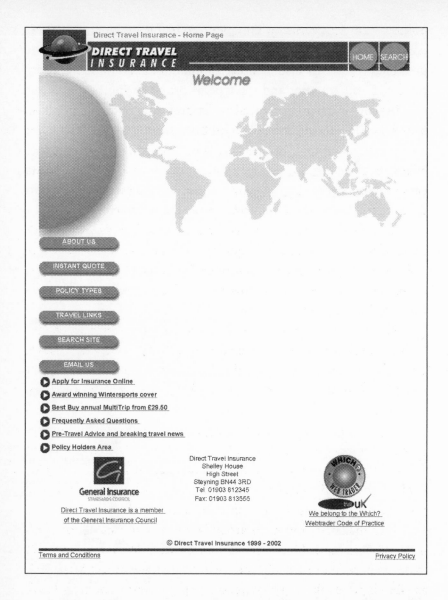

Moneyextra is impressive for its sophisticated search engine. Once you've filled in the simple questionnaire, which establishes what type of policy you're after and whether you have any medical conditions, you're given four quotes to compare plus the policy highlights, such as maximum pay-outs on medical expenses and personal liability cover. This helps you to compare on a like-for-like basis. After all, the cheapest policy isn't necessarily the best. MX

Moneyextra also gives you the option to include or exclude extras, such as personal belongings and winter sports cover, and see how the premium changes. The ability to buy online is the icing on the cake.

Moneysupermarket is also impressive for its comprehensiveness. It sifts through over 1000 travel policies on your behalf and ranks the cheapest. As with MX Moneyextra, you're given the policy details as well as the premiums and can include or exclude personal belongings and baggage cover. It consistently throws up the cheapest prices but is let down by the inability to buy online.

Moneynet also scores highly for user-friendliness coupled with some of the most competitive quotes around. You can save quotes and return to them later if you like. The only drawback was the inability to alter the level of cover, as with the other money supermarkets, but you can buy online.

The two most competitive direct insurers I've come across are Direct Travel Insurance and World Travel Direct, mentioned above. The main advantage of using these companies is that you have a direct relationship from the start rather than going through an intermediary.

Egg offers a good website design and reasonably competitive quotes. If you buy an annual policy you get winter sports cover in the price (assuming this promotion is still running by the time this book is published). Egg credit card customers also get an extra 10 per cent discount if they buy online using the card.

Sites that help you shop around can save you more than you think. For example, I have found policies using Moneysupermarket that are more than £100 cheaper than from a high-street giant such as Barclays Bank (www.barclays.co.uk). And Thomas Cook (www.thomascook.co.uk) wins the dubious prize for quoting some of the most expensive policies I've come across. You pay through the nose for the supposed security that comes with a big brand.

But remember that price isn't everything. The cheapest policy may not necessarily be the best. Check out the small print to see what level of cover the policy offers. For example, anything less than £1 million cover for medical expenses isn't really enough. Also, the money supermarkets are very good for standard policies but not as good for non-standard risks such as people over sixty-five, or who have medical conditions such as diabetes.

Ideally, any insurer you choose should offer a twenty-four-hour emergency helpline and be a member of the Financial Ombudsman Scheme. For general information about travel insurance and travelling abroad, try the Association of British Insurers (www.abi.org.uk). You can download a free leaflet, but you need Adobe Acrobat Reader (www.adobe.com) to read it.

Here are some other sites for you to try. You can buy online with all of them:

CGU Direct	www.cgu-direct.co.uk
Columbus Direct	www.columbusdirect.co.uk
Endsleigh	www.endsleigh.co.uk
Preferential	www.preferential.co.uk
STA Travel	www.sta-travel.com
The RAC	www.rac.co.uk
Trailfinders	www.trailfinders.co.uk

9
Tax

Introduction

For most of us, tax on our investments isn't really an issue because we simply don't make enough in profits to worry the taxman! For those who are wealthier and more successful, this chapter runs through some of the ways you can shelter your investments from tax and looks at some of the online tax advice sites that are currently available.

Tax on investments

There are two ways the Inland Revenue likes to eat into our investments: **income tax** on dividends and **capital gains tax (CGT)** on profits. This is on top of the mandatory 0.5 per cent **stamp duty** we pay each time we buy shares.

Dividends are paid to you with tax already deducted, so basic-rate taxpayers don't have to do anything else. But higher-rate taxpayers still have more tax to pay and so have to declare gross dividend income in their annual self-assessment tax return. The rules are quite complicated and forever changing, so if you receive a lot of dividends ask your accountant for advice. Don't forget that you will also have to declare any interest earned on cash in your brokerage account.

The second way you can pay tax is on the capital gain you make when you sell your shares. Roughly, capital gain is the current value of your shares minus the cost of buying them. CGT is charged at 20 per cent and 40 per cent, depending on your total income level. But the amount of gain liable to CGT reduces the longer you hold on to your shares. This is called taper-relief and results from the Government's desire to encourage long-term investment over short-term speculation.

Again, the rules are complex so seek advice before filling in your tax return. The Inland Revenue provides a useful introduction to CGT on its website (www.inlandrevenue.gov.uk/pdfs/cgt1.htm). You can either read the leaflet online or download it in PDF format (this type of file requires Adobe Acrobat Reader available from www.adobe.com).

Luckily, not many of us have to worry about CGT anyway because there is an annual tax-free allowance – for the 2001–2 tax year we can make £7200 gain on our shares without having to pay any tax at all. And if you make a capital loss during the tax year, i.e. if you sell your shares for less than you paid for them, you can offset this against any future gains to reduce the overall CGT bill.

Protecting your investments

We can avoid the spectre of tax altogether by sheltering our investments in a number of legitimate ways:

INDIVIDUAL SAVINGS ACCOUNT (ISA)

This tax-exempt savings account was launched in April 1999 as a replacement for the Personal Equity Plan and Tax Efficient Special Savings Account (TESSA). The main difference with the ISA is that there is a wider choice of eligible investments, including foreign shares, cash and investment-based insurance products. The annual investment limit is currently £7000. Any income and capital gains made within an ISA are tax free.

Opening a self-select ISA with an online broker is a good idea if you intend to trade seriously. One of your shares might perform spectacularly, netting you massive profits. Within a self-select ISA you wouldn't have to worry about CGT at all. This gives much greater flexibility and freedom to buy and sell at times that suit you rather than the taxman.

You can use the broker finder engine on FT Your Money (www.ftyourmoney.com) to see a list of brokers offering self-select ISAs. Just watch out for the annual administration charges, though – they can sometimes wipe out any savings you make on the tax, especially if your shares aren't big dividend payers anyway.

EMPLOYEE SHARE SCHEMES

These are schemes that allow employees to buy or receive shares in their company in a tax-efficient manner. The two main schemes are the Savings Related Share Option Scheme and the new All-Employee Share Ownership Plan. The rules are quite complex, so for more information go to the Inland Revenue website (www.inlandrevenue.gov.uk).

ENTERPRISE INVESTMENT SCHEME AND VENTURE CAPITAL TRUSTS

Tax breaks for higher-rate taxpayers investing in high-risk funds that back small and developing companies.

Online tax returns

The Inland Revenue has been encouraging us to file our tax returns electronically in an effort to cut costs. The take-up of the service has been a little disappointing, largely because the Revenue has constantly fiddled with the way they want us to do it. Once you've registered for electronic filing and received your security codes, you can complete your return online and file it via the Revenue's site if you like. If you don't manage to complete it in one sitting, you can save it and come back to it later. Get your return in before 30 September and the Revenue will also calculate your tax liability from the figures you've supplied.

If you want to do your own calculations, but still need help, there are a number of Revenue-approved services available to help you calculate your tax liability, fill in the return and file it electronically or by post. For a full list, have a look at the self-assessment section on the Revenue's website.

Digita's Taxcentral (www.taxcentral.co.uk) is my pick of the crop because it lets you complete your return online or offline. Its TaxSaver Deluxe software costs £29.99. Another software provider worth checking out is e-Taxchecker (www.e-taxchecker.co.uk). Its package is even cheaper at £19.99, but is only suitable for people with very simple tax affairs.

Online tax advice

The internet is helping many employees, self-employed people, contractors and small businesses to manage their tax affairs more efficiently and cheaply. Although accountants are gradually incorporating online elements into their services, there are very few that have embraced the internet wholeheartedly. A select few have.

ASCOT DRUMMOND (www.ascotdrummond.co.uk).

This is an excellent service that makes the most of the internet's potential. You send off your paperwork to them, which they copy, scan and put online on your own secure password-protected section of its website. They can then prepare your accounts, income tax and VAT returns, send off invoices and generally do all the usual back-office chores that make running a small business a headache. You can access your site whenever you want, see all your documents online and get an up-to-date snapshot of your financial position, including the amount of tax you owe. You are also allocated an account manager who is available by phone. The services costs from £75 a month (plus VAT) for a single person and sound like heaven for busy sole traders and contractors.

SJD ACCOUNTANCY (www.sjdaccountancy.com)

This is another firm that offers a high degree of online interactivity. Although we're a long way from the paperless office, the internet is a very useful mechanism for capturing data and processing it much more efficiently. That means SJD can take on more clients and offer them lower fees.

Clients can complete their own timesheets and expenses spread-

S J D Accountancy
Chartered Tax Advisers and Accountants
Freephone 0500 152 500

Visitor
Register Now

sheets on a monthly basis, e-mail them to the accountant and receive draft accounts back by e-mail for approval. The entire relationship can be conducted online. Many clients also scan in their bank and credit card statements, then e-mail them to the company.

The service would cost around £300 a year plus VAT for a sole trader and £720 plus VAT a year for contractors. SJD is currently developing its website to allow direct input of client data, but has no intention of handling all the paperwork like Ascot Drummond.

If you don't necessarily need a full accountancy relationship but are prepared to pay for answers to specific tax questions, **Tax Café** (www.taxcafe.co.uk), **Grant Thornton** (www.grant-thornton.co.uk) and **Virtually Anywhere** (www.virtuallyanywhere.co.uk) provide such services. You type in your question, flash the plastic and receive your tax advice by e-mail.

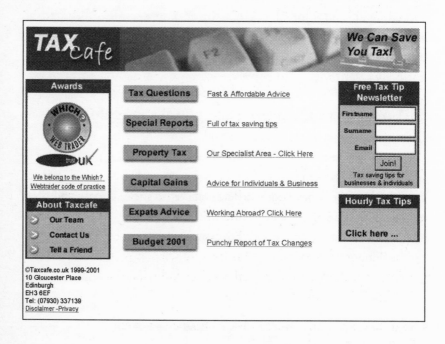

10

Regulation and Security

Introduction

In this final chapter we look at how the online investment world is regulated and how your investments are protected from theft and fraud. I'm happy to say that this is a short chapter because the dangers and risks to investors are pretty minimal. Also, the regulatory regime was simplified in December 2001, making things a lot more transparent.

Regulation

The Financial Services and Markets Act 2000 finally came into force on 1 December 2001. Brokers and other investment firms that were regulated by the Securities and Futures Authority are now regulated by the Financial Services Authority (www.fsa.gov.uk), the unified regulator for the whole financial services industry.

The FSA has four main aims:

• maintaining confidence in the UK financial system

• promoting public understanding of the financial system

- securing the right degree of protection for consumers

- contributing to reduce financial crime

New complaints procedure

A new complaints procedure is now in force. If you have a complaint against a broker or any other investment-related company you have to approach them first and give them an opportunity to sort things out. If you remain unsatisfied you can contact the Financial Ombudsman Scheme (www.financial-ombudsman.org.uk).

The new ombudsman scheme will bring together the eight existing dispute resolution schemes covering financial services. All the current schemes to be replaced by the FOS will operate under the day-to-day management of the FOS and are based at:

Financial Ombudsman Scheme
South Quay Plaza
183 Marsh Wall
London
E14 9SR

The unified ombudsman is empowered to make binding decisions based on what is 'fair and reasonable'. This means there is no longer any separate arbitration option available, but you are free to take the matter to court if you still feel hard-done-by. The service is available to private individuals and businesses with an annual turnover of less than £1 million.

There is an excellent comprehensive step-by-step section 'How to complain' on the FOS website. It is well worth a read – forewarned is forearmed!

New compensation scheme

The FSA has also set up a new compensation scheme that is the responsibility of the Financial Services Compensation Scheme Ltd.

(FSCS – www.fscs.org.uk). It can pay compensation to eligible consumers if any of its member firms breaks the rules.

The compensation limits are:

Deposits – maximum £31,700 (100 per cent of £2000 and 90 per cent of the next £33,000).

Investments – covering when an authorised investment company goes bust taking your money and investments with it, and when you lose out through poor investment advice or bad investment management: maximum £48,000 (100 per cent of £30,000 and 90 per cent of the next £20,000).

The money that is used to pay compensation comes from charges levied on authorised firms. There is no charge to investors who claim on the FSCS and you don't need legal or professional advice to make a claim.

Protecting yourself

Although there are laws to protect investors, 'caveat emptor' should still apply. It's still better not to get into a bad situation in the first place. So here's a checklist of questions you should ask before doing any financial business online:

- Is the web address correct? It may look right, but a hyphen here or a dot there can make a big difference. Ring up the company and double-check. Bear in mind that a website address that includes '.co.uk' or just '.uk' doesn't necessarily mean it's based in the UK. As such, it may not be authorised. No authorisation means no compensation.

- Are the phone numbers genuine? Check them.

- Is the company properly authorised? You can check against the FSA's register (www.fsa.gov.uk/register/main.html), now called 'Firm Check Service'.

- If an investment company is promising a very high level of investment return, is it realistic? If in doubt, seek independent financial advice. Generally speaking, if a deal looks too good to be true it probably is.

- When dealing with foreign companies do you know what your rights are under the host country's laws? Find out before committing your cash.

Security

The main point to make is that buying and selling investments online is as safe as, if not safer than, buying and selling via any other medium. The transactions and personal details are encrypted using 128-bit encryption technology that is virtually impossible to crack. It is unlikely in the extreme that hackers would be able to intercept and decode your details while they were in transit across the web.

Most broker security systems are similar, using passwords and personal identification numbers to protect your account from unauthorised access. You obviously have to keep your security details secret otherwise you could forfeit your right to any compensation should someone manage to run off with your money.

Be especially careful when using a public computer to access your investment account. If you fail to log off properly before leaving the desk, you may unwittingly be granting someone else access to your account. Again, this would probably constitute negligence in the eyes of your broker and you may not get any compensation.

The investment companies have to pass rigorous security tests by the regulator before they are authorised to conduct investment business online. These include keeping audit trails for every transaction that an investor makes. Having said that, it is a good idea to print off any contract notes or agreements just in case. Brokers also have to provide a telephone-dealing back-up service should their internet service break down.

Anti-virus software

Everyone transacting on the internet should buy anti-virus software (see Chapter 2) and keep the virus definition files updated. There are nasty viruses, worms and Trojan Horses around that can do terrible damage to the files on your computer, and possibly steal your passwords and other security details. I can't stress the importance of this enough. If you leave your computer unprotected while using an open network you are asking for trouble. Serious traders who spend long periods online should even think about going one step further and installing 'firewall' software for added protection. With a little common sense and application, investing online should be perfectly safe.

Index

analysis), 114
Moneyfacts, 154
Moneynet, 143, 149–150, 158, 163
Moneysupermarket, 154, 163
monitor size, 11
Morethan, 158–159
Morgan Fleming (J P), 116
Morningstar, 126
mortgages, 149–150
  brokers, 150–152
Motley Fool UK, 38–39, 60–61, 112
motor insurance, 157–159
moving averages (technical analysis), 114
Multex Investor, 96–97
multimedia software, 28–30
MX Moneyextra, 45–46, 61, 153–154, 162–163
myBroker, 79–80

N
Nasdaq, 94, 97, 103
Nationwide, 146
Netscape Navigator, 19, 20, 21
New York Stock Exchange, 103
news resources, 26
  sites list, 26–28
  US (United States), 95–96
  see also information, investment
newsgroups, 25–26
newspapers, company financial information in, 34–37
Northern Rock, 148, 149
Norton Anti-Virus, 16
Norwich Union, 116, 161
Nothing Ventured, 80–81, 139

O
Ofex, 71, 102–103
ombudsman, financial, 172
Online Life Insurance, 155–156
Opera, 19

options (derivatives), 130–132
overseas investment see international investment

P
passwords, and security, 17, 61, 174
PCs, buying, 10–13
PDF files, 30, 135, 166
pensions, 133–134
  Self-Invested Personal Pensions (SIPPs), 57, 137–139
  stakeholder, 133–137
performance indicators see company performance indicators
personal finance
  banking, online, 144–149
  car insurance, 157–159
  credit cards, 153–155
  home insurance, 159–161
  internet, benefits of, 142–143
  life insurance, 155–157
  mortgages, 149–152
  personal loans, 152–153
  travel insurance, 161–164
  websites, 134, 143–144
personal loans, 152–153
Personal Pension Management Ltd, 139
PINs (personal identification numbers), and security, 17, 61, 174
plug-ins, 28–30
portfolios
  diversification, 84–85, 108–109, 128
  fantasy, 49–50, 70
  monitoring, 49–50
precautions, prior to online transactions, 173–174
price/earnings ratio, shares, 36
printing
  contract notes, 20, 63, 174
  web pages, 20